FEMININE RISING

Experience Your Life in a New Way

CATHY ENOCH

BALBOA.
PRESS
A DIVISION OF HAY HOUSE

Copyright © 2015 Cathy Enoch.

All rights reserved. No part of this book may be used or reproduced by any means, graphic, electronic, or mechanical, including photocopying, recording, taping or by any information storage retrieval system without the written permission of the author except in the case of brief quotations embodied in critical articles and reviews.

Balboa Press books may be ordered through booksellers or by contacting:

Balboa Press
A Division of Hay House
1663 Liberty Drive
Bloomington, IN 47403
www.balboapress.com
1 (877) 407-4847

Because of the dynamic nature of the Internet, any web addresses or links contained in this book may have changed since publication and may no longer be valid. The views expressed in this work are solely those of the author and do not necessarily reflect the views of the publisher, and the publisher hereby disclaims any responsibility for them.

The author of this book does not dispense medical advice or prescribe the use of any technique as a form of treatment for physical, emotional, or medical problems without the advice of a physician, either directly or indirectly. The intent of the author is only to offer information of a general nature to help you in your quest for emotional and spiritual well-being. In the event you use any of the information in this book for yourself, which is your constitutional right, the author and the publisher assume no responsibility for your actions.

Any people depicted in stock imagery provided by Thinkstock are models, and such images are being used for illustrative purposes only.
Certain stock imagery © Thinkstock.

Print information available on the last page.

ISBN: 978-1-5043-4284-1 (sc)
ISBN: 978-1-5043-4285-8 (e)

Balboa Press rev. date: 11/20/2015

Contents

Expressions of Gratitude vii
Preface xi

Section One: The Inner World Vs. The Outer World 1
    Chapter One: Beginning our Exploration 3
    Chapter Two: The Feminine – Our True Essence 10

Section Two: Beginning the Healing 19
    Chapter Three: Expanding Our Experience of Her 21
    Chapter Four: Forgiveness 36
    Chapter Five: It is In the Release We Find True Expansion 49

Section Three: The Feeling Tone of Spirit 59
    Chapter Six: How About Those Feelings? 61
    Chapter Seven: Divine Decisions 72

Section Four: Moving Forward 77
    Chapter Eight: What if We were All Right? 79
    Chapter Nine: Where can We Go from Here? 84

Practices:
    Love Meditation 16
    Practice a Non-Judging Meditation 28
    Practice a Non-Judging Prayer Time 30
    Forgiveness Meditation 47
    Feelings Meditation 69

Expressions of Gratitude

Sincere offerings of love and gratitude...

to my mom and dad. Once loving and dedicated parents, you are now great friends to me, and at-the-ready confidants. You have been amazing teachers throughout my life. I am so grateful I have always felt loved and cared for by you. I love you so much.

to my first spiritual teacher, Rebecca Moravec. Your time here was a blessing to so many. From your teaching I learned to be fearless in the realm of Spirit, and confident in my experience of it. You taught me to see with my heart, and helped me awaken to a quality of Love I had not known existed. It was in me. It *is* me.

to Erik & Cheri Knuth, and the UB Wellness Institute. Erik, you helped me find the stillness within, and you taught me how to create stillness within my body. Your work is a true, pure yogic experience. There are *some* gifts I might offer to only a few because I think it would suit them. The Unified Body Method you created is a gift I would offer to everyone, so that all might have a taste of this delicacy. I wish your Unified Body Wellness Institute great success.

to Deepak Chopra and Eckhart Tolle. Your teachings have spurred many a quantum leap in my understanding as I've explored my way through this spiritual journey. My gratitude for your work is beyond words. Thank you, Tom Galten, for offering your lectures on, and introducing me to, the works of Eckhart Tolle. Wow!

to Schlitz Audubon Nature Center in Milwaukee, WI. Your Spiritual World of Nature Series extends your loving and gentle footprint on this Earth into the realm of the Eternal. Excellent and beautiful work, Don Quintenz.

to Karen Balistreri. You introduced me to the concept of consciously living an abundant life. Why did I ever believe it was supposed to be hard? You are a gracious and generous teacher.

to Dr. Lisa Stewart, the brilliant and beautiful senior pastor of Spiritual Living of Greater Milwaukee. I am very grateful for the important work you share. You created a loving space for me to work out my inner revealing. You offered good counsel and encouragement as I squeezed myself out from under the paradigms that did not serve me. I was not part of your congregation when you graciously opened your abundance class to all. Much gratitude for your generosity in giving.

to Mary Manin Morrisey, for your wonderful course called Prosperity Plus...A New Way of Living. You introduced me to the expanded life, and guided me to the realization that 'my thinking was too small for the Life that was seeking to express itself as me'. Mary, what comes next *is* what I would LOVE to do.

to Sondra John, Independent Graphic Designer, and amazing friend. The gift of your art for the cover has draped these pages with a perfect vision of expansion. Your immediate belief in this work was an inspiration to my heart. Yours is the kind of deep friendship I had always hoped to be the other half of. I am blessed.

to Dann O'Connor, whose editing skills you, the readers, will be as grateful for as I am. Should you come across any grammatical discrepancies, know that Dann will have done his best to bring me into compliance with known "best practices". Thank you Dann, for the untold hours of work and focus you gifted to this work. You have the seasoned eyes that allow you to see from the perspective of the unknowing. Sharing that gift with this work has made it so much better, just as sharing the gift of your friendship has made my life better.

to all those teachers, guides, and wise ones who have offered me innumerable and important life lessons. I am grateful for each of your gifts. And, I welcome those teachers yet to come into my life, who will offer to teach me more of what can be.

Preface

Before reading this book, I'd like you to have an understanding of my spiritual perceptions around the masculine and feminine aspects of our shared experience on this Earth. I will also share how I define some of the concepts I'll be relating to in the book. This way, as you come across them, you will have a foundational understanding of where I'm coming from.

The Feminine and Masculine

It is my perspective that, spiritually, we all possess perfectly balanced aspects of the feminine and masculine. They are inexorably linked, and therefore absolutely equal in importance. They are also an integral part of us all.

I consider these perfectly balanced feminine and masculine aspects to be innate facets of God as well. Because of that, anytime I refer to an aspect of God in this book, I will capitalize that word, whether it is regarding the Masculine, or Feminine. So, when you see "She" capitalized, it does not mean I am trying to make the point that God is a woman. I personally do not perceive the Divine as either sex. I see the Divine's expression here on Earth in a multitude of ways. Two of those ways have been labeled "masculine" and "feminine" by us.

That said, you will notice I am directing my words towards women in this book. My reason for this is because something in me is saying there is work for us women to do. This work will allow us to experience our True Essence, an important part of which is the Balanced Feminine aspect of the Divine. This is *our* work to do, and we do masterful work when we do it consciously.

Our work with the Feminine will impact the Masculine in a profound way. It must, as they are inextricably, energetically intertwined. So, while this book may seem focused on women, I cannot emphasize enough my tremendous appreciation of the Masculine. When I speak of one, I am ultimately speaking of both.

Our True Essence

What I mean by "our true Essence" is that thing many of us call the spark of the Divine, or spark of the Holy Spirit. This spark offers to encompass our entire way of being as we allow It to expand within us, and express Itself through us. The very fact that we call it a spark indicates our current limiting belief in its purpose, and impact. I now realize it is much more expansive than the name we have given It.

As Mary Manin Morrisey shares in her <u>Prosperity Plus Series</u>, "Our thinking is too small for the freer, fuller, expanded Life that is seeking to express Itself through us." This Life is our very essence. It is who we are, in reality.

The problem is, we have not been taught this Essence is our reality, so we aren't experiencing ourselves in this way. All the glorious, wise, strong, victorious, amazing ways we have always wanted to be, are in fact, who we already are. Our desire to be those things has been coming from deep within us, from the Divine Feminine who *is* all of those things. She has been calling for us to wake up to Her, and experience ourselves in all Her extraordinary ways.

She has been whispering to us in ways we've never recognized as Her. Her voice has been in that warm breeze we love as it gently brushes our hair back. Her voice has been in the heart-melting giggle of a baby. When our spirit explodes within us as we stand in awe of a sunset, Her voice has been there saying, "This is Me. This is how I feel. Look for Me! I'm here!"

Unfortunately, we have been conditioned to tune out that voice. That's the reality we've been told to ignore. But we can wake up, and pay attention to that voice anytime. As we do, we will find that still small voice, like the spark, isn't so small either. When we begin to listen, and follow Her to what is within us, we will have a whole new world to explore. We will have found our guru, and She is us.

The Concept of Powers vs. Energy

In some circles, the terms feminine power and masculine power are used freely, with the understanding of its spiritual implications. However, power remains one of those words that carries with it a lot of preconceptions. Among other things, it tends to incite our inner competitor, so throughout this book I will refer to the powers possessed by either the masculine or feminine, as *energy*. I believe the word energy inspires a keener sense of the unseen, and the subtle yet amazing strengths we all have in our natural states of balance.

A Note from My Heart for the Wounded

For those who have been harmed or damaged by people we would call evil, this book may challenge your current sensibilities.

If you think I am wrong about something, I would ask that you let me be wrong. Let it be my perspective that differs from yours, and continue reading. Find what is in this book that *is* for you. Your work is sacred. No one can tell you how you should live with your experiences, or how to work out your own healing.

When we experience very challenging conditions in our lives, it can be difficult to even consider the concept of a Loving God. My wish for you then, is rest. Take a breath when you can. The rest of us are holding space for you, surrounding you with love, whether you feel it or not. And if you don't want it, that's okay. It is not intrusive. It is simply offered every minute of every day, there for your taking whenever you wish.

SECTION ONE

The Inner World Vs. The Outer World

CHAPTER ONE

Beginning our Exploration

We are about to go mining for spiritual gold. Similar to miners who seek the vast veins of precious metals beneath the earth's surface, we will venture beneath the surface of our current experience to find a hidden life within us.

This life I speak of is in every one of us. Like the grand arteries of gold, the obese lakes of oil, and gargantuan stores of natural gas beneath the outer layer of earth, there is an extraordinary life happening within us. It coincides with, but plays out very differently from the life we are experiencing at our surface. This extraordinary life, like all the precious materials beneath the surface of our earth, is there, whether we mine for it or not.

I say, let's go mining.

We'll be boring through layers of our current existence, challenging belief systems, transcending the ego, and releasing our hold on limiting illusions. As we shed old paradigms and expand to new ways of thinking, we will be inviting this inner life to rise up in us. It will begin to flow through the channels created by our journey to the center of our being.

There are countless names we can give this Inner Life - God, Spirit, Allah, or even Enlightenment. We use such names to effectively point to what we are referring to so that others may understand us. So, in this book, I am calling this Inner Life the Balanced Feminine. To add variety, or perhaps to direct your focus, I will also refer to this Life as the Divine Feminine, God, Spirit, or simply She or He. In keeping with the mining theme, consider my words the lanterns lighting the way on our expedition.

Releasing a Limiting Illusion

As women, we have gone through phenomenal changes at our outer level over the last 150 years. From the early woman's rights movement, to the feminist movement of the 60's, we have been exerting our external abilities in powerful ways.

But there have been unintended consequences to our working mostly from this external level. I would like to briefly explore this part of our current experience.

The feminist movement was absolutely necessary. It was a movement crucial to our growth as women, and as a nation. It was also a step toward our spiritual growth. Although the feminist movement was so very important, it was however, a grab for the wrong power.

It was a power grab for male power - more specifically, though unintentionally, for *unbalanced* male power… or, as I wish to refer to it, unbalanced masculine energy. We *had* to reach for that masculine energy. It was the power we identified as being stronger.

We were wrong about that. Although unbalanced masculine energy *was* dominating, *balanced* Masculine energy never was, and never will be stronger than our own balanced Feminine energy. Before we start getting too puffed up, our Feminine energy isn't stronger than the balanced Masculine either. They are different aspects of the One Source, completely, and implacably linked to one another.

Chapter One: Beginning our Exploration

One of the features of the feminist movement that I find interesting is that, as part of our rebellion, we were insisting on being treated as equals. And so, we set out to be equal to oppressive, dominant, self-absorbed, competitive driven, testosterone-fed egos. (Take a breath guys. I love men. You get a much better rap later. I'm trying to make a point here.) I don't suppose that's who we really wanted to become, but looking around, we kinda did.

We had certainly wanted to rise above being treated as "less than", in the home as well as the workplace. We wanted to be freed to choose our life path, and pursue our heart's desire. We wanted to be heard, to be validated, valued for who we were, not for dutifully fulfilling our given gender role. Something within us was collectively inspired to become more. And look at what we did. We became a lot more. Boo rah.

Taking a look at where we've gotten, there are certainly many successes and failures at the individual level. Taking a wider view though, we can see something doesn't quite fit right.

Our forays into the corporate world did not coincide with balance in our family life. How many women are working the 40-90 hour work week, *plus* attempting to manage most or all of the home duties? Caring for the sacred home was something our moms and grandmothers dedicated their entire days to accomplishing!

Many of us are on anti-depressants, visiting therapists regularly, stress eating, or self-medicating. We are plopping ourselves in front of the television as a means of shutting the world out whenever possible. Many women feel some level of guilt, inadequacy, or exhaustion regarding the raising of their children.

Some of us have struggled with the climb up the corporate ladder. Could it be an indication that something isn't fitting when so many of us who *are* viewed as successful in business are also labeled "bitches"? Let's be honest. That moniker is not always handed out because the men don't want us there, or other women are jealous. Sometimes it's just true, and some women will tell you that's what they had to become to succeed in the business world.

I would argue that these experiences have some truth to them precisely because we are attempting to live in the space we created from the hijacking of someone else's energy.

So woman, get real honest with you for a moment. What best describes your experience of this life so far:

> Walk in the Park,
> Living the Dream,
> Uphill Climb,
> Never Ending Treadmill, or
> Trudging Through Mud.

Enter a proxy vote here for your friends who can't slow down enough to even read this book.

Thank God for those who were able to say "Walk in the Park" and "Living the Dream". There is an energetic wake created by those having such life experiences. As more people live their dream, that energetic wake expands, making it easier for others to join them.

That conscious stream of "Living the Dream" is what we're meant to be experiencing. The only reason we are not doing that is because we do not know, or believe that is truly our intended and natural state of being.

Men/Women and Masculine/Feminine

We have grown quite accustomed to making distinctions between men and women. We've written endless books about this in hopes of figuring each other out. We make jokes about these differences, go to counseling over them, and yet the sexes often remain at odds with each other.

And so much of the time, as we couple in our unbalanced states, one of us becomes "less than" within that relationship. Some become less than who they were before the relationship. Others become less than they want to be, and less than they would have been if they had chosen a partner from a place of strength and balance.

We all know people who choose relationships that seem unhealthy for them. Some of us *are* those people, or have been. It breaks our hearts to see those close to us in destructive, debilitating relationships. We know in our innermost being, there is something better. *They* also know it or wish it could be true themselves. This is all part of the twisted dance that we call, "The Differences between Men and Women". It is the best we can do in our current state of imbalance. In this space we remain separated, unknowable to each other.

Moving Beyond the Stereotypes

I am not going to list all of the positive and negative attributes of the stereotypical man, and stereotypical woman. We know them. Quite a lot of us live them. That's why they are called stereotypes. But women, our True Essence is *so* much more than our very best day as a woman. And men, your true Balanced Masculine Nature is *so* much more than your very best day as a man. There is work to be done, healing and revealing to take place, so that we can experience the balanced aspects of ourselves.

Our perception might be that we would then reach a higher place. But the reality is, as we slip into this exquisitely fitting life of balance, we will simply be experiencing our natural state of being, the way we are intended to experience life.

How *easily* we slip into this exquisite life will look different for each of us. How willing are we to let go of the patterns that no longer serve us? How easily can we relinquish old paradigms, and embrace new, expanded ones? It's a process, shorter for some than others. No process is better or worse than another, just different. I wish for each of us that the process would take only moments to complete, but if it were to take years, it would be worth every moment of time given.

A New Perspective

There is another way of looking at "us". As mentioned in the Preface of this book, it is my perspective that we all have within us the perfect balance of the Masculine and Feminine energies. At the level of Spirit, we are experiencing that perfect balance all of the time. Our work is to awaken to this reality, and allow it to become our experience on the physical plane.

For those of us here as women, we might be drawn to invite the Feminine to rise up, knowing that will allow the Masculine in us to come into balance as well. Others may be drawn to explore the Masculine within, and allow Him to rise up, knowing the Feminine will find Her balance in this way. There is no recipe one of us can give the other. Each of us has the voice of God speaking in us, ready to guide us on the way that suits us best.

Imagine each of us as an aspect of the Divine Essence that is God. That would make you The Divine Essence of God expressing Itself here on Earth as you, and I would be the Divine Essence expressing Itself here on Earth as me. The Essence of God is expressing Itself here as every man, every woman, every animal, every tree, and every drop of water.

If we accept that God is present in *all* things, then we are each fully an expression of the Divine Energy that is God. Our truth within this understanding is, there is only harmony between us all. This is our intended way of being.

Chapter One: Beginning our Exploration

When we view each other as a fully connected, endless network of Divine energy, we respond to each other very differently than when we view ourselves as separate, different from, and competitive with one another.

At the level of Spirit we always meet each other from this place of connectedness. We are doing this every day, all day. We simply don't experience this because we are not functioning from our True Essence. We have forgotten how to access it, how to live from this place.

We have too long lived within the illusion of being separate from one another. It really is just a belief system we have bought into, and a story we then collectively continue to write. We can step beyond that illusion anytime. When we are open to new perspectives, there's no telling what new understandings we will experience.

The purpose of this book is to bring awareness to the Feminine aspect within us. To awaken us to Her qualities, Her desires, and Her greatness within each of us. I offer signposts for those who wake up to Her and choose to find out all this can mean for them.

As we do this work we will experience the rising up of our own wise, strong, healing, compassionate, steadfast, creative, and loving Balanced Feminine Energy. As our authentic energy is realized, we will release our hold on the unbalanced male energy we latched onto during our feminist revolt.

Our letting go of that unbalanced energy is crucial. It will allow the amazing, effortlessly supportive, righteously defending, healing, mentoring, and loving Balanced Masculine Energy to rise up as well. In *this* space each of us may fully realize our natural state of being, and our life experience will look quite different.

CHAPTER TWO

The Feminine – Our True Essence

> *Therefore, the master acts without doing anything, and teaches without saying anything. Things arise, and she lets them come; things disappear, and she lets them go. She has but doesn't possess; acts but does not expect. When her work is done, she forgets it. That's why it lasts forever.*
>
> Tao Te Ching

So, we understand the experience many of us are having is not our intended way of experiencing life. That's why it feels so difficult. It doesn't fit! Life shows us this lesson in the simplest of ways, if we just pay attention. As one example, when a piece of clothing fits perfectly, it is easy to put on, easy to wear, and we feel great in it. Right? So how does your life fit? Easy to put on every morning? Easy to wear all day? Do you feel great in it? Does that seem too mundane to count as a lesson for life? Well guess what, it can be just that easy.

For those who don't love the way their life fits, there *is* another way of being here. The Divine Feminine always feels good to "put on". It might not feel quite normal at first, but we can't help but feel good as we align ourselves with Her, or "put Her on". As we become attuned to Her, our intuition is expanded to a new level of knowing. Simply bringing Her to our awareness begins to attune us to Her promptings.

As you read this book, recognize Spirit speaking to you through the feelings you experience. You may feel something resonates with you, or you might experience a sudden warming in your heart. There may be a rush of inner excitement, or a longing. All of these can be Spirit telling you to pay attention. The Divine Feminine gives clear signals when there is something for you to take in or explore. And, when something doesn't resonate with you, allow that to mean it is not for you, at least not at this time.

Our spiritual work can be done more clearly when we pay attention to these kinds of inner promptings. You really aren't imagining these promptings. At least not in the way we generally define imagining. I will write about this more later.

What Does She "Look" Like?

There are many aspects of the Feminine. One of the first places I began to recognize Her was in the book written by Clarissa Pinkola called, <u>Women Who Run With the Wolves</u>. (An excellent read. Bring a steak knife; it's meaty. Deliciously juicy and meaty.)

Having gotten a taste of the Wise Woman within me, I opened myself to understanding more about the Balanced Feminine and Masculine energies. I began to experience the Divine Feminine within me more and more, and continue to do so. I will share some of my insights so that you might readily recognize Her in you.

Words for describing the Feminine are really just signposts for announcing when we are in Her presence, or perhaps as a marker that we are not. But a caution: These words are not meant as flashcards indicating how we should be attempting to behave.

Words such as compassion, peaceful, love, etc. are not suggesting a benchmark of behavior for a given instance.

Those words instead, will be describing what the Divine Feminine brings with Her as she rises within us. It is how we will experience ourselves, because this is who we truly are. We just haven't been experiencing Her because we haven't been looking for Her. We've been too busy flailing about in this unbalanced masculine energy that doesn't fit us.

So as we seek Her, open ourselves to Her, and awaken to Her, we will begin to experience Her rising up within us. Like getting a new wardrobe from the inside out. And it fits perfectly.

This journey to our authentic selves will look different for each of us, but always beautiful. I urge you not to judge how quickly you experience any particular aspect of the Feminine. Just do the work and allow for how She reveals Herself to you.

In the following pages, I will describe some of the ways She has revealed Herself to me. Again, these descriptions are meant as signposts to help you recognize Her until you begin to trust your own experience of Her.

Wisdom of the Ages

There is calmness to the Divine Feminine because She carries with Her the understanding of the whys and whats. She sees the foggy layers keeping us from experiencing our true Nature, and She offers love. The depth of Her love can reach around the world and beyond, to offer healing. She speaks beyond ego, acts with confidence and poise, and laughs with abandon. She dances with wildness, inwardly or outwardly, as She chooses. She fully celebrates the joy and success of others. She embodies the understanding of the ancients. She walks in the stream of connectedness with all things, and quite easily creates an abundant life.

These are all qualities we can experience as we explore, and allow for our understanding of this aspect of ourselves. This is who we are in the balanced state we are intended to live this life.

Compassion

Love is one of those very over-used words. Much like the word God, love comes with much baggage. So I am inclined to find other words that will allow for a truer understanding of what I wish to convey regarding this aspect of the Feminine. I will start with the aspect of love called compassion. Many of us have lots of that now. But in our unbalanced state, it can cripple us because we feel so badly about the tragedies around us, and in the world.

In the realm of the Feminine, compassion coupled with wisdom brings a strength that can inspire us to action. And not necessarily to physical action. We can do amazing work energetically as well. We can find our way to this energetic work as our understanding expands.

This compassion coupled with wisdom is felt for everyone. We may be accustomed to feeling compassion for victims, the oppressed, and the like. But it came as a surprise to me, that when I felt my very strongest connection with Spirit, I would experience deep compassion for the people I was accustomed to feeling anger towards. The bad guys, the criminals, those who take advantage of others, the "perpetrators of evil". In my deepest heart I found myself realizing how far removed they were from experiencing *their* True Nature. My heart would ache as I pondered how far they must be from experiencing God's love to be able to perpetrate such horrific acts.

Having compassion for those, who some would call our lowest angels, does not diminish the compassion offered to their victims. Conscious compassion for all, both villain and victim brings with it the vibrational frequency of healing. Something hatred and anger have never accomplished. And, every mindful parent will tell us we can still punish bad acts with conscious compassion.

This may seem beyond understanding, and in our unconscious state, it is just that. Remember, I am not encouraging you to begin *being* this way. You need not argue with this point of view, or try to understand it. As we allow the Feminine to rise within us, we will experience Her compassion in our hearts as it is meant to be experienced.

Mindfulness

Being fully present is one of the most magnificent gifts we can offer ourselves. There are amazing experiences that can only be known in this space called mindfulness. We do not create this space by being mindful, we join that which always exists within, and around us. It is the person we *think* we are, meeting who we *truly* are, our Divine Essence. And of course, the Balanced Feminine dwells here, so whenever we are living mindfully, we are aligning ourselves with Her. It is here we experience Her grace, stillness, knowing, peacefulness, and joy. We are not feeding our soul in this state of awareness. We are being introduced to it.

In our current cultural climate of rapid-fire multitasking, it can be challenging just to take a conscious breath, let alone concern ourselves with remaining fully present in each moment. Our minds cannot conceive of it. Luckily, we are not asking this of our minds. The work of mindfulness, ironically, has almost nothing to do with our mind.

When being mindful, our only instruction regarding the brain is to pay no attention to the constant chatter it produces. We don't have to try to quiet the mind. We simply ignore its rantings, reminders, and judgments. Let any thoughts become as the "Wah, wah, wah, wah" teacher of Charlie Brown animation fame. Our attention is elsewhere, experiencing each moment from the perspective of our Divine Essence, our True Nature. We are Spiritual beings having a human experience. We are now exploring what that means, observing our human experience from this place of stillness, and waking up to the extraordinariness of our True Self.

It is not to say we will all be transformed in a single moment to a full understanding of, and abiding in this mindful state. In our current state of collective *un*consciousness, it may take practice for us. Meditation is where many turn for this work. We are shifting paradigms here. Chosen quiet times allow us to become accustomed to hearing what Spirit sounds like, and what experiencing even brief moments of the Balanced Feminine feels like. As we attune ourselves to Her voice, *She* no longer remains the "Wah, wah, wah" in the background. The voice of Spirit becomes clearer, recognizable, and familiar. We can then remain mindful more often throughout our day. We learn to trust this new way of experiencing our life. The Divine Feminine proves Herself to be real.

To be clear, our beautiful minds have not been discarded. This work also enables the rewiring of our communication system between Spirit and mind. This, of course, is a crucial part of the mind, body, and spirit balance long recognized as necessary for enlightenment. So you see, we're not letting go of our mind. We're letting go of the ego running the mind, and returning that skill set to the Source of the mind's creation.

With much gratitude I share this meditation taught to me by Rebecca Moravec, my spiritual, and Reiki teacher. This meditation has helped me experience the Divine in a profound way.

Love Meditation

Sit quietly and allow your breath to slow to an even, easy pace. Bring your awareness to it. Allow your breath to fill your lower lungs so your belly rises instead of your chest. Do this the best you can, but if this is very new for you, do not get hung up on it.

Now, begin surrounding yourself with love in whatever way works for you. Perhaps bring in beautiful green, or soft rose light that fills every cell of your body. Or, picture yourself floating effortlessly in the clouds, surrounded by angels sharing their love with you.

Perhaps think of Jesus, or Mother Mary gazing at you with great compassion, or holding you in their loving arms. You might imagine yourself sitting in your favorite place in nature, and allow the trees to shower you with leaves of love. Or, picture a waterfall filling you with love.

Create any image that allows you to feel love being administered to you. Surround yourself with this love. Take it in. Take it in until you're swimming in it. Then, when you've had a good long fill of this love, begin sending it out to the world, to the Earth and all its inhabitants.

Enjoy this for as long as you like. Before getting up, take a moment to feel the gratitude that is within you. Whenever we spend time with Spirit, there will be a deep sense of gratitude. It is profoundly worthwhile to enjoy some time with this feeling.

A note on breath work - When we get our breath down to our lower lungs, we will experience a sense of relaxation that our shallow breathing does not offer. Breath work is a very helpful practice. To get accustomed to "belly breathing", try lying on the floor and putting a light book on your belly. Then, breathe with the intention of making that book rise. Be mindful that you are not just using your stomach muscles to make the book rise.

This practice also offers us an opportunity to exercise the virtue of patience. Many of us resist working with our breath at first, but those who stay with it are always grateful.

SECTION TWO

Beginning the Healing

CHAPTER THREE

Expanding Our Experience of Her

We spend billions of dollars in our modern society trying to understand ourselves, find healing, attain balance, and experience wellness. We seek the assistance of therapists, yoga instructors, spiritual leaders, books, and the list goes on.

Reaching out for support and assistance on our path of expansion is not a bad thing. It's that we are doing so without real direction. We are looking for something or someone to follow. We want to get to another level of understanding, and experience sustained peace in our life. We take this class, read that book, follow that teaching. Something inside of us knows there is more than what we are experiencing. So we set out to find that thing we are missing, that elusive key to our awakening.

We've been trained to look outside of ourselves for this kind of work. It's not that this is the wrong direction, but it is the longer route. We will remain on this Toll Way of Spiritual Seeking until some part of our outer work takes us within. The key to our awakening has always been within each one of us.

You have within you, right now, everything you seek. I am calling this the Divine Feminine. What name will help *you* recognize It?

Call it your Inner Teacher, the Holy Spirit, Allah, or your Higher Self. The words don't matter. How the *right* word or phrase makes you feel is what matters. Which name makes you feel excited, hopeful, stronger? The one that rests in your heart like it belongs there is the one for you. You recognize it. Don't get hung up on the words. They all point to the same Thing. In our collective state of imbalance we just aren't agreeing with what to call It right now.

But here, we are bringing our awareness to our expansive Inner Guidance. So, which word makes you feel connected to something real?

Now, I know we women get a bad rap for feeling too much. Some of us have been given a lot of conditioning that we're not to trust our feelings. There is an important distinction to be made here between emotions, and feelings. More on that later. What I am speaking of here are the feelings we experience when we see with our heart. This is a much different experience from the emotional response our body has to our wildly shifting thoughts. Not experiencing or trusting our intuitive feelings has not been serving us well.

Here's the thing. When we look inward, and consciously connect with our Inner Guidance, we can learn to walk confidently on our path. We get our information directly from the Source, and we know it with an unshakable confidence.

From this place we won't be tossed about with the unbalanced emotions we tend to experience when we're winging it. It can take some practice as we get acquainted with, and gain a deeper understanding of, the Essence that dwells within us. Here are some simple guideposts to experiencing this.

Be Honest With Yourself

If you pray, be honest. It's not as if God does not already know what you are thinking. How can we feel intimate with anyone we are hiding our truth from? Hiding is so unnecessary. There is only Compassion and Love offered to any of our prayers.

There is never a barrier put up by God, whether we speak our truth in prayer or not. So if you're mad, speak it. Mad at God? God already knows. Speak it! Sorry you feel mad? Speak that too. You are emptying your heart for *your* sake, and God will always fill that space created, with Love.

When we harbor things that we judge unspeakable, we close our hearts to some extent. We can still pray in this state, and I would encourage it, but we limit our experience by restricting our willingness to accept Love. All because we came to our time of prayer judging ourselves, our acts, our thoughts, or our worthiness.

Some might say we cut ourselves off from God by judging others. I believe if we weren't first judging ourselves, we would not then be passing our judgments onto others. Everything about us is known by God. And still there is only an abiding, irrevocable, expansive Love being expressed within us, toward us.

More Places to Practice Honesty with Ourselves

As we journey into the spiritual realm, we are often doing so in groups. We go to classes, workshops, places of worship, book clubs. Here we share our experiences with others, and our egos come with us. What if we are not experiencing as much as everyone else says *they* are? What if we aren't grasping the concept being taught? That makes us feel flawed or inferior, and our egos really hate that.

One way to override that feeling of inferiority is to speak your truth. Honestly share your lack of understanding, or your different experience. Trust me; you will not be alone in perceiving things differently from the greater group, even though you *may* be the only one speaking that truth. Share your truth, and you will have become a teacher to the others in the room. Perhaps they will be emboldened to share their differing experience as well.

Just as important, you will have opened yourself to truth, your truth. That is a gift to celebrate. Stand in that space, and feel the strength there. That is the Feminine rising in you. I didn't say it would feel comfortable at first. Your ego may not like it. But, speaking your truth will always feel freeing, and that's the feeling you pay attention to. That is expansion.

As we practice honesty with ourselves, we learn to trust our intuition more. We can begin to hear, feel, and experience that Inner Knowing. It may feel as if channels of communication are being opened up. Truth has a way of creating space. As we begin to experience that sweet spot of the Spirit more often, we can then learn to trust how we make our choices when seeking spiritual support. It can serve us well to reach out to those who are called to teach, counsel, or write books, when we are guided by Spirit.

When allowing our Inner Guidance to point the way, we can trust when we are drawn to something. That drawing feeling is our Inner Guidance saying, "Yes. Let's do that. There's something here for you". (Note that word "feeling" again.) When we choose to seek the help of others from *this* place, it is from a place of strength, not weakness. It is knowing where we need to be, even if it's just an inkling of knowing at first. That sense will get stronger as we listen to It.

Be Open

There are paths, dimensions, and spiritual revelations we haven't yet begun to glimpse. Exciting, fascinating, expansive understandings yet to be ours. When we keep our hearts and minds open to what Spirit has to reveal to us, it is like opening up *all* the doors and windows of our home on the perfect spring day. That beautifully fresh, warm breeze clears away the staleness. Don't we *feel* raised up by the freshness of that sweet spring air? Hopeful, excited, blissful, peaceful, contented! Any and all of those feelings is Spirit tapping us on the shoulder, revealing Itself to us, saying, "This is Me. Here is how to recognize Me. I feel *this* way."

There is nothing to fear when we keep ourselves open. We simply need to set our intention of being open to only the Divine. We can call on God's protection from anything that is not for our highest good. When we do that, there is no chance God's protection does not come. So then, regardless of our individual beliefs of what "evil" may lurk in the realm of spirit, we can be confident in our Protector. We can now feel safe doing our inner work; open to whatever Spirit has to show us.

In the realm of Spirit, we are all completely and freely dwelling within the Love that is God. That realm exists within us constantly. We are never separated from this, never. The fact that our current experience appears differently from that is only a testament to our current beliefs.

What illusion have you accepted as your current truth? Perhaps you don't believe you *can* access that realm, don't deserve to experience it, or think you need to earn it. Or, maybe you don't believe it exists at all. We are welcome to keep our belief, hold on to it if it feels like a good fit. But, if or when it doesn't, we need only open our minds and hearts for Spirit to show us something more. That's when it really gets interesting.

The revelations, understandings, and how they come to us, can be extraordinary when that is what we are open to. Allow for awesome, and you will get awesome. God will show us who we are in whatever way we are ready to experience it. When our intention includes understanding the Divine Feminine aspect of ourselves, this too will be revealed in precisely the right way for each of us. We only need to remain open.

I have never felt as cared for as when the Divine has revealed something expressly for me. Something so specific to my given situation, there was no explanation but that I am constantly in the presence of The All Knowing. That understanding was followed by the whisper of Spirit saying, "I know you. I am part of you. I am with you every moment. Spend time with Me, and I will show you more of what that means."

You are not relegated to, and need not be content with intimate but ephemeral experiences with God!

The Divine Universe is always revealing Itself to us. God is not hidden to most while parceling out answers to secrets among the esoteric elite. We are all meant to fully experience our oneness with All That Is. This would include freely communicating with All That Is. Here again, it is only our limiting beliefs that restrict this intended flow.

Do your personal work in bringing down the barriers between you and your communication with the Divine. Be open to this communication being more than you have believed it could be. Let it be the magical, instantaneous flow of inner understanding you would love it to be. Then, all you have to do is to start paying attention. Inspiring moments may be infused with a personal revelation for you. Nature will provide innumerable messages, lessons, and understandings, when we are open to them.

Look at it this way. The universe is God's mailbox. In it, is an open invitation to experiencing our intended way of being. We only need open that mailbox in whatever part of the universe we are willing, for our own understanding of this to be revealed.

God is absolutely everywhere, so wherever you feel inclined to get your counsel, God is there. God reaches out to us in whatever way we are most able, or willing to hear. That's why some are called to be rabbis, ministers, teachers, or gurus. We very often need to start hearing from the Divine at this physical level, through others.

We can then grow beyond the milk of our teachers, going within to expand our level of understanding. We have this Inner Teacher. As we listen to the promptings of this Higher Guidance, we learn to trust in That which is within us.

Now, from *this* place, we can choose to reach out to others for spiritual nourishment with an inner knowing. We can offer spiritual nourishment to others as well, knowing we are still here to help each other on our journey. That inner knowing is the Feminine rising within us.

Free Yourself from Self-Judgment

Judgment; this word also carries baggage. It feels heavy, doesn't it? Another feeling to consider. But this feeling is *not* hopeful, peaceful, exciting, or loving. If we follow from the earlier concept, then this heaviness would not be of the Divine Feminine. It may feel very familiar, but it doesn't feel expansive, and this is your clue.

Let's briefly explore what self-judgment accomplishes on your behalf. Then, determine for yourself if you wish to retain it as a tool for your growth.

Meditation

Have you ever tried meditating? When you've realized for the fifth time that you were reviewing your grocery list, the kids' schedules, or whatever else, what comes next is crucial. If you judge yourself for having yet again lost your focus, are you more, or less likely to continue in your meditation? Better to laugh at yourself. Allow for your distraction, without judgment. Give it no mind, and continue with your meditation.

This is the practice that will, in time, become your natural response to the mind's incessant chattering. You really don't have to concern yourself with stopping the chattering when you are paying no attention to it.

Being free of self-judgment also means not chastising yourself if you are only able to stay with your meditation for a few minutes. There is absolutely no benefit in giving energy to thoughts of frustration, or condemnation when you stop your meditation one minute after you sit down.

As you practice *not* spending time with frustrated, angry thoughts, you will find the next meditation easier to sit with, and the next easier yet. Pretty soon you will be able to continue your meditation without getting mad at the dog when it barks, the neighbors for starting their car, or the phone ringing. Whenever we stop giving our attention to the thoughts that arise during our meditations, we create space for expansion. We always have a choice of what thoughts we pay attention to. Exercising that choice is an excellent practice.

Practice a Non-Judging Meditation

The only thing you want to accomplish during this meditation is focusing on your breath. Your practice will be allowing for thoughts as they arise.

The breath-work we will be doing is focused on eliminating pauses between each breath. You may be surprised to realize you've been holding your breath in between inhalations and exhalations.

Sit quietly. Close your eyes, and focus on your breath. Keep your awareness on the breath coming up into your nostrils and the breath going out. When your lungs are filled with air, consciously let

the breath begin going out without pausing. When you've taken a full breath in, simply relax to allow the breath to be released without a pause. Notice when your lungs have emptied, and begin taking in the next breath without a pause.

The practice begins when thoughts arise. Instead of reacting to them, you simply allow them to be there. No judgments about them at all, no energy given to making them go away. You simply return your awareness to your breathing whenever you realize you've been carried away with a thought.

As the next thought arises, you simply return your awareness to your breath. No matter how often a thought gets your attention, you go back to the breath, without judgment.

Should you find yourself feeling frustrated, bring your awareness back to the breath, without judging yourself for feeling frustrated. The moment you realize you've begun criticizing yourself for having gotten carried away by a thought, go back to the breath. Focus on the air coming up into your nose, and keep your awareness on the air being slowly exhaled. Feel your lungs empty.

Do this for as long as you are able. If this is only for 45 seconds, do not judge yourself. Simply allow that to be your fully performed practice for that time. It is all perfect.

Take a moment to feel the gratitude within this experience.

Prayer

We talked earlier of not speaking our truth when praying, but some of us have different challenges we bring to prayer. I'd like to address another of them here. Have you struggled with praying? Do you get frustrated because you are so easily distracted? Do you try to push aside your complaints and your negative thoughts? If so, ask yourself, does any of this help you feel the Love of God? Are you strengthened?

We do not need to spend a bit of energy trying to push thoughts away, argue with them, or judge ourselves for having them. All of this only distracts us from experiencing God.

It would be like calling your best friend on the phone, and instead of conversing with them, you began talking with yourself, grumbling how crummy your hair looked that day, or that the hem of your pants was torn. Then, frustrated with all your annoyances, you hang up on your friend, never having shared a true moment with them.

But we generally don't do that when we call a best friend. Those thoughts might come to mind while we are on the phone, but we ignore them while we are talking with our friend, and address them later if they matter enough.

Let it be that way when you call on God. Simply ignore any thoughts that aren't part of your conversation with God. Your blessed conversation occurs within the Stillness that exists beyond all thought.

Practice a Non-Judging Prayer Time

Before beginning this prayer practice, take a few moments to formulate your prayer plan-of-action. Seek your own best practice, but here is one idea pulled from our daily life experience.

What do you do when you are enjoying a television show, and commercials come on? Fast forward past them? Get a snack? Talk to someone in the room with you? Whatever it is that you do, try finding some way of translating that to your prayer time when those distracting and judging thoughts come up. So keeping that in mind, let's give it a try.

In this scenario, you are watching television, and have no means of preventing commercials from interrupting what you are watching. So, what would you do when they come on? Would you fast-forward past commercials? Okay, translate that to your prayer experience. When judgmental thoughts arise, envision a remote control that you press to fast-forward past those thoughts.

Would you get up to get nourishment? Good. When in prayer, have a favorite Bible verse, or book passage to recite each time a distracting thought has grabbed your attention.

Would you talk to someone in the room during a commercial? (This is my personal favorite.) Envision Jesus sitting beside you, and have a little laugh with Him over your distracting, or self-judging thought. As soon as you are wondering if you left the garage door open, or are clicking through your day's schedule, picture Jesus tapping you on the shoulder. Maybe He's clearing His throat, or flicking the side of your head with His finger to bring you back to your conversation with Him. Then smile, or laugh with Him about it, and move on. Experience the lack of judgment from Him each time.

If this is all you do for an entire prayer session, it will be inspiring and strengthening. You will have witnessed over, and over again, the pure Love of God. Your imaginary head might be sore from all the finger flicking required to get your attention back to Him, but it will be worth it.

Mantras

Some people include a mantra with their quiet time or meditation. Mantras are sacred utterances with great spiritual meaning. I won't go into detail here due to my limited experience with mantras, but the practice includes repeatedly saying a meaningful word or phrase, silently or aloud. For staving off judging thoughts, I can certainly see how using mantras could help.

By keeping the mind's main focus on the word or words being repeated, any other thoughts attempting to rise up would be more easily allowed for. Thoughts then become like soft music playing in another room. You know it's there, but it's not loud enough to dance to. So, choosing a mantra to work with could be a great practice for anyone wishing to tune out your "monkey mind".

I could go on describing how judging ourselves thwarts our attempts at a deeper spiritual experience, but I'm hopeful I've sufficiently made that point. When we judge ourselves we constrict, we retract, we feel removed and separate. None of that is life-giving, expansive, or useful.

Let part of your practice be choosing *not* to judge yourself wherever you have been doing this during your spiritual endeavors. So, if you don't experience what you think you should during a spiritual workshop, accept this as the experience you were meant to have. When you cannot walk a straight line during a walking meditation, bring your awareness to deep within you, and ignore the ego wishing to grade your walk. When you sense the judgment arrive, find your way to dismiss it. It does not serve you.

I found *my* way one day as I was watching a beautiful stack of clouds above me. It occurred to me that I never attempted to change the clouds I was viewing, because I had no expectation that I *could* change them. If I did not like the clouds overhead, I simply waited for them to pass. If I liked the clouds I was watching, I enjoyed them. A voice inside me said, "You can't stop thoughts from coming into your mind any more than you can change those clouds. So just allow them to pass. Spend no energy trying to change the thoughts, or make them go away. Just allow for them."

Once I accepted that I could not stop thoughts from coming, I also stopped judging myself *for* them coming! This was huge for me! Freeing, expansive, exciting!

Another layer to this lesson was offered on a different day. I noticed a crow chasing after a Red-tailed Hawk. The hawk was clearly bigger than the crow. Yet, as the crow relentlessly picked on the hawk, a behavior called "mobbing", the hawk, for all intents and purposes, ignored the crow. It did not engage the crow or try to make it go away. The hawk is not as agile a flier as the crow, I am told. It seems then; the hawk has the wisdom to know it can't make the crow go away. Thus, it gives no energy to attempting to do so.

I had seen this bird behavior before, but on this day it hit me like someone had slapped my forehead. I am not able to keep random thoughts from coming through my mind during my meditations. Like the hawk, I can't make them go away. So, don't put any energy into trying to do so. And those thoughts include judgment. I can't stop those judging thoughts from coming either, but I do not have to give them any of my attention. They are just crows.

This was a beautiful, and welcomed bolstering of the earlier understanding I'd gleaned from the clouds. But Spirit wasn't done with me on this subject yet.

This message from the hawk and crow was deepened by showing up in other aspects of my life. Like with the driver who wouldn't let me in to change lanes - just a crow. I couldn't do anything about that person's behavior, so why react to it? Or, the little bombshells thrown into my day by others - just crows.

It wasn't long before it hit me that it wasn't those *people* who were the crows. It was my *thoughts* about those people, and situations that were crows. I didn't have to pay any more attention to those thoughts than the hawk did regarding the crow.

When I was successful at not getting carried away by those thoughts, I realized I was suffering less. I was no longer participating in judging those people, those situations, or myself. I did not let thoughts steal my peace. The practice of not judging myself, or others, became a more normal part of my experience, and that allowed for growth in new ways.

In the realm of Spirit, and spiritual growth, negative judgment regarding one's experience only hinders both. Find your way to dismiss self-judgment. You may be amazed at how this practice alone will shift your experience of this life.

Slow Down

A good friend of mine has a decorative sign hanging next to their door so she and her husband are reminded each day before heading out, "Don't run faster than your Guardian Angel can fly". Now, we all know Guardian Angels have no trouble keeping up with us, but how many of us are moving at lightning speed all day, every day?

One thing I've found is, when I move at lightning speed I have more difficulty hearing Spirit. Going that fast through the day drives my awareness up into my head, fully engaged with thought. And I can tell you, when I'm running that fast, what's happening in my head is not pretty. There is an endless juggling of tasks in my brain, running through lists of what hasn't been done yet, what puzzles haven't been solved, what she needs, and what he needs.. What's worse is how I'm *feeling* about all of that craziness. It can be downright painful.

The time came when I recognized I was afraid to slow down enough to *try* to experience the peace I desired. I feared if I didn't keep my focus up in my head I'd drop some of those balls I was juggling. Sound familiar to anyone? That is not what a balanced life looks like, I promise you. And we don't have to live that way.

We can release these frantic patterns, and embrace a new paradigm, a new way of being in this world. I call it the Wise Walk of the Balanced Feminine. Allow Her to rise up in you. She knows when to move, and when to sit quietly. She offers Her intuition for what is of real value to be done, and what is to be let go. The peace-filled confidence She brings to our walk affects absolutely everyone around us.

She naturally, and without apology, cares for Herself. She knows this is necessary. It teaches Her children, and other women, their own worth by observing how She honors Herself. She speaks Her truth with strong wisdom, love, and compassion.

As we acquaint ourselves with these qualities rising within us, we can accomplish extraordinary things, in a way that does not deplete us. We can do work that serves us, and others without ever taking energy away from another. We are able to move gracefully in our world. And, we can make new agreements with what we want our lives to look like. Thank God, we can slow down. In *that* space, we may experience another way of creating, beyond the constant motion of physicality.

CHAPTER FOUR

Forgiveness

Our current human version of forgiveness tends to be very constipated. We know we should forgive this or that act, this or that person. We are told our healing will come with forgiving. Some of us just don't want to forgive. What that person did, or what *we* did is just too horrible to forgive. Others want to be able to forgive, but can't find a way to get to that place in their heart.

In Spirit, forgiveness is instantaneous. It may take us a while to allow for that kind of forgiveness, but the Balanced Feminine within us will bring this with Her. Like compassion, we will know forgiveness as we are meant to, as we open ourselves to this expanded experience.

Forgiving Your "Self"

For many of us, this needs to be a starting point. And for many more of us, this thing called forgiveness can be an important component to our spiritual healing and growth.

I am not talking here about any specific religious teaching, such as that in the Bible which speaks of the forgiveness Christ offered at the cross, although as a display of true authentic forgiveness, it stands alone in its awesomeness. Even if you are not a Christian, you can recognize the Divine in a man dying at the hands of others, and forgiving them with compassion because, "They know not what they do".

What I *am* talking about is the full on, loving forgiveness we can offer ourselves, and each other.

In this modern era, we have truly done our woman-selves a disservice in the department of guilt. As we donned our feminist suits, and joined the business world, we did amazing work. We were breaking through barriers, and overcoming discrimination. In general, we were roaring and warring our way in the corporate world.

As our successes mounted, the dust began to settle. Soon, we shifted from fighting for change to living within the change we had accomplished. It wasn't that our work for change was completely done. We are *still* pushing against a glass ceiling, and wanting equal pay. But with each generation there were more of us joining the business world as a matter of course.

Perhaps this is when the guilt began to seep in. We were no longer pulled by the great cause of equality. Nor were we reveling in the accomplishments achieved by those great lionesses of the woman's movement. We had now begun our struggle with balancing home and job.

The collective energy created by our feminist movement was so strong that we *all* felt we were supposed to join the workforce outside of the home. We began to feel we were less than other women if our desired vocation was to raise our children. Add to that, our intense interest in keeping up with the "Joneses", and a whole lot of us who wouldn't have chosen work outside the family took on second and third jobs.

Adding insult to injury, we began lying to each other about how our home and job balancing act was going. Had we been honest with one another from the start, we might have learned more from each other. But, after generations of hiding our truth, women continue to step onto the speeding treadmill that is working mom, and expect to do it all...with ease.

As a symptom of our insanity, we have made it a point of pride to run this hard. These wonderful working moms will give seemingly every waking moment to kids, job, husband, and home. And one day, maybe at 35 or 55, she will have run herself into the ground. With a smile on her face, she will lift her head up from the mud, and mutter, "I love my kids", while the rest of us applaud her.

Let me define this mud we find ourselves face-down in. It is heart disease, diabetes, fibromyalgia, depression, addiction. We might say we can do it all, but the one very important thing we so often do not accomplish is caring for ourselves. There is Spirit-loss to this kind of living. We don't lose Spirit, we lose experiencing It.

For those who *have* kept their title of stay-at-home mom, it may have taken a little longer, but look how insanely busy *their* schedules have become. Could it be they are unconsciously justifying their choice by living in as much chaos as their counterparts in the business world?

Many of us are running in such an unconscious state that we are oblivious to any inner longings, or to any signs warning of us of upcoming mud holes. Those women would be the ones rebuking my prior description of the speeding treadmill; they are ones saying to themselves that they are doing just fine, and handling their lives very well, thank you.

Splat. Applause.

What seems to come along with so many of us, regardless of our life choices, is a healthy dose of guilt. We don't feel we are doing enough, being enough, doing well enough, doing as much as other women. It's possible, one of the reasons we're running so hard is so we don't have to look at this part of our picture.

Chapter Four: Forgiveness

We can heal from that state of being. And we don't need to go back to the 1950's to do it. We weren't our authentic selves then, either. As we wake up to the Balanced Feminine within us, we will begin to explore all that this means for us. And it will look different for each of us. In our new and growing sisterhood we will welcome these differences. We will be joyful for all of our individual successes, unlike the current state of our scrappy womanhood.

As mentioned earlier, for many of us, this healing needs to begin with forgiveness, starting with our individual selves. I'm not suggesting you forgive yourself for working too hard, or not working hard enough. It is not about forgiving any of the things you've done that, if you *could* look at them, would require forgiveness.

Start with forgiving this false self you have believed yourself to be. Forgive this human who has been walking through life with your name. She has been unaware of her true Divine Essence. Forgive her for that. *That* self has just been managing this life the only way she knows how. She didn't know how to do any of it differently, or she would have. Remember Jesus said, "...they know not what they do". That is literally true for each of us.

Until we wake up to who we really are, we are doing the best we can to navigate within this world. We are steeped in the illusion that we have no other means of navigation. This illusion is like having to fly a plane without a control panel. With no control panel, there is also no headset for communicating with the control tower for assistance. We are all alone in this thing.

Now, some of us would somehow navigate their way to a safe landing. Some of us have literally done that! Others might just jump out of the plane. And a whole lot of us would crash land, with varying degrees of severity.

Would you judge yourself if you found you had to fly a plane with no prior instruction, and no help? Of course not. Yet, we constantly judge ourselves, and others, for how we attempt to navigate our human existence without the use of our control panel (Intuition), or control tower (Inner Guidance).

To illustrate this, imagine you as a passenger in an airplane (life), just enjoying the ride. But, the ride begins to become bumpy, the plane pitching dramatically (challenges in life). There is no one around to ask what is happening.

When it seems this flight (life experience) is continuing to deteriorate, you go looking for answers. You get to the cockpit, and find no one is there. You are going to have to start flying this plane (gain control of your own life). Oh, and there is no control panel. So, what are you going to do?

You *could* remain in a state of panic, and wait for the inevitable crash and burn. Or, consider that you have another option. You can realize with such certainty that this scenario is so completely insane, that some part of it just cannot be true.

In *that* moment you would ask yourself, "Who would make a plane (life) without a control panel?" That wouldn't make any sense at all! Something about this cannot be true. So now, you look for that control panel (seek your intuitive truth). There *must* be some lever to pull or button to push so the control panel will rise up from the floor.

And in that moment of believing that there *must* be a control panel, you are able to see it clearly sitting in front of you. Not only that, but the headset that connects you with the control tower is securely on your head, and you know exactly how to fly this plane.

That, my friends, is called a paradigm shift. We have thought there is only one way to fly this thing, this life, and *that* is an illusion.

In the previous scenario, why didn't you see a control panel when you first stepped into the cockpit? Because I *told* you there wasn't one, and you went along with my story; you believed me. Life is very much like that. We have collectively accepted certain aspects of our existence as truths. But are they?

Chapter Four: Forgiveness

For generations, maybe eons, we've been passing down the illusion that we are separate from our Creator. Loved by, watched over by, or perhaps at the mercy of, but always separate from, God. Something about this cannot be true if we also acknowledge that God is absolutely everywhere.

We've also been told we have only this brain with which to navigate our experiences in life. Every single aspect of our lives is run by and through this three pound mass of gray matter within our head. Something about this cannot be true. It fails too many of us, too much of the time. As phenomenal and intricate as this three pound wonder is, we spend endless dollars trying to figure out what has gone wrong with it. And seriously, where *is* the mute button?

Having been trained into these concepts of separateness from God and exclusive navigational rites to ego, we come into adulthood with a particular way of seeing this world; of how things work, what we can expect, and how we can be in it. That's our plane ride.

When our lives start getting too bumpy, pitching dramatically, and deteriorating beyond hope, many of us start looking for answers about why this ride is going so unsatisfactorily. We go looking for these answers outside of ourselves because we've been taught we are passengers on this ride called "life".

Well, we are not passengers. We are the pilots. And not just pilots, but highly skilled pilots. We possess perfectly honed instincts, the wisdom of the ancients, and all of the faculties required for navigating our lives, skillfully. Once we wake up to this realization, we can begin the exploration of accessing those faculties.

This is a paradigm shift, to be sure. A spiritual "fracking" of core beliefs, with the space created instantaneously flooded with the light of the Divine.

This shift will look different for each of us. It may be a process of releasing, and expanding. Releasing old patterns and limited thinking, and expanding as new understandings emerge. Inklings that lead to questions, becoming revelations.

Perhaps at this point, you *have* inklings there may be some other way of navigating your life. Begin to explore this. Look within, and ask what there is for you to understand around this concept.

Whether you are ready to begin that kind of work or not, do your self a kindness. Forgive your self for flying your plane in whatever crooked, crazy, going in circles way you've been flying it. You've been flying the only way you knew how.

And all of it, all the things this world would call mistakes, bad choices, bad acts, or the things we would put ourselves down for, have been ushering us toward our waking up. Whenever we begin our *conscious* work to learn, experience, and understand what Spirit has to teach us, we realize all these things have been steps toward our growth. So, forgive your self, and thus begin your healing.

The Law of Forgiveness

There is a beautiful law regarding forgiveness. Whenever it is offered up, there is a freeing that takes place. The one doing the forgiving ignites a magnificent, clear channel of loving energy. The one accepting the forgiveness steps into this beautiful stream of breathable, loving energy. There is healing in this space, and a clear path on which to move forward.

In the context of forgiving your self, as much as you can, spend time in this stream of forgiveness. You will be the initiator of this forgiveness, and the one stepping into the circle of loving energy. Allow for what happens. Experiencing the Divine in you, forgiving the you that has been trying so hard, can be incredible, and profoundly moving.

At the level of Spirit, forgiveness and love are always being offered. We just need to go within to experience this. There is no safer place to be. There is no judgment in this space. You don't have to look at anything you don't want to; you can simply be in this space, experiencing freedom from judgment, and the peace-filled stillness that freedom brings.

Spend some time here, and one day, maybe the very first day, you will experience loving your self, this human who misguidedly thought she had to run this whole life by the seat of her pants. You will realize she had not been trained on all the tools she had come into this life with. Of course you can forgive her.

In the moment you understand this, you release your judgment of the job you've been doing. Compassion replaces criticism, love replaces loathing. A freeing of your soul has taken place. This will be the Feminine rising in you. Allow for Her healing. There is expansion here.

When you have fully integrated this paradigm shift, you may begin seeing others a bit differently. When you see the crooked, crazy, going around in circles way they are flying *their* lives, you will understand it is because they do not yet know how to do it differently. They have not been trained on all the tools they came into this life with either. No wonder there is such chaos in our world.

Forgiving Others

From this place of expansion we can, whenever we feel the desire or need, begin offering this authentic forgiveness to others. As our awareness of the Feminine expands within us, doing this can become a very natural part of our experience. We then experience our part in creating that magnificent, clear channel of breathable, loving energy. Now, when we forgive others, we invite them to step into this space with us.

They may not be interested in our forgiveness, or they may not be here anymore to even ask for our forgiveness. But remember, there is a law to forgiveness. Whenever it is offered up, there is a freeing that takes place. The freeing takes place *at the offering*. So, as *we* stand within this clear channel of love to forgive whatever has been done to us by another, *we* are healed. They may, or may not join us in this space for their own healing, but our healing is guaranteed. With our own healing realized, we can move forward freely, carrying no baggage regarding that situation.

And that can be a clue for checking the authenticity, or completeness of your work regarding forgiveness. Check to see if you are moving forward freely, or if you are dragging some baggage about the situation behind you. If you aren't sure, then presume you have baggage. We may have grown insensitive to the loads we carry, but we will always feel the glorious weightlessness that comes from being free of them.

Sometimes forgiveness may need to happen in layers, so once again, don't judge yourself if some baggage remains as you begin this work. You may find that, even when you thought you *had* forgiven yourself or someone else, it comes back at you some other time. Allow for this. Go within to see what is meant for you to understand. There is good work to be done around it or it wouldn't be back for another round.

You will find as we begin to walk in the light and wisdom of the Balanced Feminine, we no longer complain about why we have to deal with something that has come up. At least we will begin to do so less often. It can be a process. More and more we learn to welcome what comes, knowing it is for our highest good. We intuitively realize there is something there to learn, know, or experience toward our greater understanding.

We can welcome it because we have a deep sense of knowing we are completely cared for, and have within us the means to successfully understand, and navigate what is before us. We are opening to our intuition, and our confidence in it grows as we work with it.

Keep in mind; I am not suggesting you should *try* to respond in these ways. I am describing attributes the Feminine will bring *with* Her as she awakens in you. This *will become* your experience. Perhaps not all at once, or perhaps it could happen in an instant; don't put God in a box. And remember, one experience is not greater than another – just different. Remain open, and allow your experience to be what it is, without judgment.

Forgiving a Moment or Situation

When faced with challenging situations, we very often spend a lot of energy resisting them. We may not even be aware of how much energy is being used wishing we didn't have to deal with whatever is happening. We don't realize how we deplete ourselves with being angry and stressed about a situation, even as we go headlong after our solution. So we rail against the situation, and then agonize over what to do about it. This might explain why we are so tired.

We have another option. Although it may take some practice to start from this place as situations arise, it is an option well worth exploring. Forgive the situation, and look within for guidance. Forgiving a situation means we are allowing the situation to be what it is. We offer no resistance to it.

This is far from resigning ourselves to what is happening, which comes with feelings of hopelessness and helplessness. When we allow for what is happening, we stand squarely in front of it. If it is here, then there is something important to learn, know, or experience from it. Then, we look within, or *dive* within, to seek the counsel of our Inner Guidance, our Wise Woman, the Divine

Feminine. From this place of strength, we confidently choose our course of action.

The Space Within

This place I am directing you to go for your inner guidance is vast, and extraordinary. It is also the very essence of who you are and of all that exists. It is a place of all knowing. And, because it is part of who you are, you have complete access to it, all of the time.

This doesn't mean we will experience knowing everything that has ever been, and ever will be known. I think we humans have a *lot* more work to do in order to experience that level of expansiveness. But, it *does* mean we have full access to whatever Divine information is needed to understand, and respond to, our human life experiences.

Learning to live from within our Center, where we experience Divine communication every minute of every day, will create new lines of communication between our heart and our mind. These two aspects of ourselves come into balance through our unfettered connection with Spirit. We then seek our Inner Guidance and the Divine responds in our heart. What we know in our heart then speaks to our mind regarding our course of action, and the Spirit within us confirms with a resounding, Yes!

These experiences are so powerful. They reveal to us our true Essence, and what we are capable of knowing and understanding. Should a challenging situation arise where you *don't* go to your Inner Guidance for wise counsel, you will clearly see the difference in your experience. Perhaps you'll be able to check within afterward, to see how you would have dealt with that situation differently had you sought your Inner Guidance.

Doing this is strengthening to our spiritual practice as well. It is all part of deepening our understanding of this aspect of ourselves, the Divine in us. We are attuning ourselves to Her. Each time we *do* successfully bring our awareness to the Inner Feminine, we anchor our understanding of Her. We witness how She moves in our world, how She allows for what is before us, and how She responds with a foundation of love.

Forgiveness Meditation

This mediation can have many layers to it. At some point, while sitting in this space, you may decide there is specific work you wish to do regarding forgiveness. It may be to forgive your self, or someone else. You may simply wish to remain open to experiencing forgiveness in whatever way is for your highest good. Sometimes, we just need to stand in the light of being forgiven.

When there is specific work you wish to do, state your intention, and then remain open to how Spirit will work this out with you.

If you have difficulty experiencing or picturing what you desire in this meditation, start with the Love Meditation from Chapter 2. Once you are drenched with love, return to this meditation.

Sit or lay quietly. Allow your breath to become even. Keep your awareness on your breathing. Feel the air drawing up into your nostrils, then release the breath when your lungs are full. Release the breath through your nose, slowly and quietly.

When you are ready, silently state the intention that you are here for the work of forgiveness. If you have something more specific, state that intention. Next, imagine a bright light beaming down from above, and shining a circle of white or gold light around you. See yourself lifting your arms up to take in this light, and then bringing your arms down to your sides again.

Imagine yourself looking down to watch this light begin to expand around you, creating an ever widening circle for healing.

When you are ready, invite into this circle the person, persons, or situation you are here to work with, even if that person is you. Picture the person you've invited now standing within this circle of forgiveness with you. If that is too intense or distracting, create a representative for that person or situation; a stand-in. Find a way for you to move forward in this process. Be patient when you are new to this kind of work.

Allow for what takes place as you stand in this space. Remain open to what you experience, knowing you are meant to clearly understand it. You are safe; you are loved, and very cared for.

If at any time you feel uncertain or stuck, return to focusing on your breath, and simply enjoy standing in the healing light surrounding you. Remember; give no energy to judging your experience. Allow yourself to be where you are. This is a practice. Just sitting to meditate at any level is good work that will create space for the next time you sit.

Before getting up, take a moment to experience the gratitude that surrounds this experience.

CHAPTER FIVE

It is In the Release We Find True Expansion

-ALUMAH SCHUSTER

Why All These Challenges?

The Feminine knows each challenge is an opportunity for growth. Without pressures many of us wouldn't seek the deeper, expanded life. We wouldn't look for Her, and She is so worth becoming. There are places, things, and ways of being we can't even fathom until we are experiencing ourselves from this balanced state. How much pressure are you feeling these days? Perhaps She is calling for you to wake up to Her. There is another way of being in this world.

In our unbalanced state, the challenges we experience are often viewed as interruptions in our lives. We have little patience for, and rarely welcome them.

In contrast, the Balanced Feminine brings with Her the wisdom of actually welcoming the lessons being offered. She also smiles a bit, knowing that many opportunities will present themselves around those lessons most important for us to learn.

As our spiritual awareness grows, we may begin to understand this pattern of challenges. We're *supposed* to learn something from a challenge, and until we do, it will keep coming back around, in one way or another. It is that important.

The trouble is, we are often still trying to figure out what these lessons are from our unbalanced state. We get the message from within that there *is* a lesson, and then use our superficial human understandings to try figuring it out.

Nothing is clear from that vantage point. We find we are not confident that we have figured out what the lesson was supposed to be, or that we've succeeded in learning it.

We have already established that such uncertainty is not a trait of the Balanced Feminine. So, when we realize we are operating from a place of uncertainty, we are recognizing that we are not aligned with Her. That is our cue to go within, and seek the part of us that knows exactly what there is to learn from any given challenge.

Remember, Her goal is to bring forth the full expression of Herself within our lives. Anytime we look within for understanding, we will find Her. Some aspect of Her will be there to reveal Itself to us as we make ourselves open to what Spirit has to show us.

We are beginning to live consciously now. Consciously aware of our connection to the part of us that knows. We experience ourselves walking with Her, and eventually being fully integrated with Her. We are One. We always have been, but now we are beginning to experience our lives in this way.

As we grow in this practice, we become very aware of the lessons learned through our experiences. Now, when a challenge presents itself in our life, we walk fearlessly forward, because we are grounded in knowing that all is well here. Any lesson being offered is one worth learning.

CHAPTER FIVE

It is In the Release We Find True Expansion

-ALUMAH SCHUSTER

Why All These Challenges?

The Feminine knows each challenge is an opportunity for growth. Without pressures many of us wouldn't seek the deeper, expanded life. We wouldn't look for Her, and She is so worth becoming. There are places, things, and ways of being we can't even fathom until we are experiencing ourselves from this balanced state. How much pressure are you feeling these days? Perhaps She is calling for you to wake up to Her. There is another way of being in this world.

In our unbalanced state, the challenges we experience are often viewed as interruptions in our lives. We have little patience for, and rarely welcome them.

In contrast, the Balanced Feminine brings with Her the wisdom of actually welcoming the lessons being offered. She also smiles a bit, knowing that many opportunities will present themselves around those lessons most important for us to learn.

As our spiritual awareness grows, we may begin to understand this pattern of challenges. We're *supposed* to learn something from a challenge, and until we do, it will keep coming back around, in one way or another. It is that important.

The trouble is, we are often still trying to figure out what these lessons are from our unbalanced state. We get the message from within that there *is* a lesson, and then use our superficial human understandings to try figuring it out.

Nothing is clear from that vantage point. We find we are not confident that we have figured out what the lesson was supposed to be, or that we've succeeded in learning it.

We have already established that such uncertainty is not a trait of the Balanced Feminine. So, when we realize we are operating from a place of uncertainty, we are recognizing that we are not aligned with Her. That is our cue to go within, and seek the part of us that knows exactly what there is to learn from any given challenge.

Remember, Her goal is to bring forth the full expression of Herself within our lives. Anytime we look within for understanding, we will find Her. Some aspect of Her will be there to reveal Itself to us as we make ourselves open to what Spirit has to show us.

We are beginning to live consciously now. Consciously aware of our connection to the part of us that knows. We experience ourselves walking with Her, and eventually being fully integrated with Her. We are One. We always have been, but now we are beginning to experience our lives in this way.

As we grow in this practice, we become very aware of the lessons learned through our experiences. Now, when a challenge presents itself in our life, we walk fearlessly forward, because we are grounded in knowing that all is well here. Any lesson being offered is one worth learning.

Chapter Five: It is In the Release We Find True Expansion

Once we value our challenging situations, and welcome them as a means to further growth, we will find ourselves allowing for these challenges when they come. It is here we begin to experience *allowing* as instantaneous *forgiveness*.

Should we initially react with our old pattern of resistance, we can shift our way of being whenever we realize we are immersed in that old pattern. Just like our meditation practice. Remember? Whenever we realize we have been carried away with a thought, we simply bring our awareness back to the breath, to within, without judgment. Now, our inner practice becomes our outer practice.

Whenever we release our resistance to what we are facing, we create space for Spirit to rise up within that space. We take our focus off our problem, bring our awareness back to the Feminine within, and listen for what is meant for us to know.

Personal Story

As I began to experience this new awareness of Spirit in me, I would find myself realizing that I was reacting to events in my life in a way that didn't really suit me anymore. Right in the middle of stressing out over a situation, I would sense inside that some part of me was perfectly at ease.

As I first began experiencing this, I would continue on with stressing out. But sometimes, after I had calmed down enough, I would look inside, and explore that other aspect of me. It felt almost as if there was another life happening within me. It was peaceful there, all the time, every time I looked.

I would even try to argue with this other life. "Why aren't you upset? I have good reason to be upset!" I would then begin listing all my rationalizations for my reaction. This would often get me emotionally worked up again, but eventually I would look inside again to check how this other part of me was feeling. Had I made my case well enough? Then I would get quiet, and honestly wait for a response.

So often, perhaps every single time, I would first be flooded with compassion. I would be enveloped by a deep, abiding love. And underneath this love, there was a tender understanding...of all of it. All of whatever it was I was bringing to this conversation.

As I was bathed in this compassion, I would quite often sob my way through the release of all the unconscious waste I had come with. As I would empty myself, Spirit would be filling me with yet more love, new understanding, and a new perception of what I had been so upset about.

It was a whole new perspective. The wisdom that came with it was amazing, and spot on. The peacefulness around it created a seat for this new understanding to sit squarely in. Like an anchor, it stuck. I also had the sense that I *could* be experiencing this peace at *my* level, all of the time. It was my natural state of being.

It was hard for me to imagine at the time how that would work exactly, but the seeds were being planted. Every time I came to Her sobbing, the seeds were watered, and She tended to them with Her compassion, and wisdom.

Soon, I developed the consciousness to start taking a look at that "other me" *while* I was stressing out. I found I could, in fact, just go there. I could stop reacting to the chaos I was experiencing in my mind, and simply be this peaceful, calm "me" that was within me.

I will admit, I felt pretty ridiculous at times. I might be in the middle of a rant, when I'd get this sense of peacefulness in me. I had a choice. I could continue my rant, or I could experience this place of peacefulness.

To stop mid-rant, and shift to a peaceful state is quite a jolt to the psyche. There is a momentum that comes with an intense emotion. This momentum has an expectation of the emotion being played out. It wants to finish what it started. Pulling the rug out from under a fit of rage can leave the psyche feeling cheated.

There were times it took a conscious act of my will to allow the rage to fizzle, while I shifted my awareness to this place of peace within me. It was not always graceful, but it was amazing. However this process looked whenever someone happened to be witnessing it, I imagine they were just happy to have the episode end. In time, I could put words to the shift, making for a more understandable transition. The words generally began with some sort of apology for my strong reaction.

This process was a little easier when I would be alone during a meltdown. I could more easily allow for the sudden shift to peace. I could also more easily take a moment to sense what I could allow to rise up from within me, from this other me.

I always really liked this other part of me. The words that would come from this place were extraordinary; wise, honest, poignant, and freakishly right on target to resolve the situation. I so loved the grace, peacefulness, and calm that would always replace my crazy. I resolved to be willing to look ridiculous any time I "woke up" during a meltdown. I was having a fair number of meltdowns those days.

The challenges I faced during that time were an important part of my journey in letting go of who I thought I was, and getting to know who I was meant to be. My succession of meltdowns gave me much practice in allowing for the Divine Feminine to show me Her way of being.

A point worth emphasizing - I had to consciously allow for this duality-chaos on one level, and absolute stillness on another. Had I judged myself during these experiences, I would have shut them down. It felt so odd. But Something told me the stillness was real, and to be explored.

As I allowed for this practice, my meltdowns became less and less frequent, for obvious reasons. Before I would reach that highly unconscious state, I began looking within to see what there was for me to understand.

At some point regarding this practice, I also became aware of that duality in other aspects of my life. I remember distinctly the first time I was feeling completely spent, mentally and emotionally. And then suddenly also realizing, some part of me wasn't feeling that way at all. I had this sense I could continue experiencing the exhausted state, or I could just as easily experience this fully energized state that was deep within me. This other me.

In this other part of me, there was unwavering strength and energy. I remember at first thinking, "If I go *there*, I'll have to keep moving forward, and I don't want to do that. I just want to sit down, and not get back up."

But the whole idea that this other place in me existed was so intriguing, I kind of peeked into it. Then, I felt ready to step into it briefly to see how moving forward from *that* place would actually feel. It felt pretty good! And kind of easy.

Now, I don't remember which way of being I chose that first time. I very well may have decided to sink into the abyss of exhaustion because I deserved the rest it gave me permission to take. But somewhere along the way, when I again became aware of this duality, I did choose this other me. I stepped out from that muck of weariness, and into this *Life* going on inside me, and in that instant, I felt renewed.

Beyond all the patent words I could include to describe that experience, like blissful, glorious, or extraordinary, what surprised me was, I could *still* then choose to sit, and rest. But, there was a completely different energy around the resting. Not so much resting, as enjoying just *being*. Well that, and getting used to how this new way of experiencing myself felt. These spiritual revelations almost always feel to me very strange, but also quite natural.

So, I could sit still in this renewed state, or if I wished, I could move forward with refreshed, clear thinking. I would do whichever felt right for me at the time. It was amazing that all it took for me to be transformed from an emotionally and mentally spent state to such renewal, was to simply bring my awareness to that Inner Life, the Divine Feminine. It was instantaneous, and as succinct as deciding to step into my house, or out of my house.

In all of these situations, each time I chose the Divine Feminine, She fit beautifully. I felt bolstered, clear, fully capable, and at peace. I felt loved, and that I *was* love all at one time. I also began to trust that *this* was how I was meant to be walking through this world.

I spent more and more time looking within, both in meditation, and as I went through my days. I began experiencing this Balanced Feminine as the authentic me. Instead of consciously going *to* this place, I was finding myself coming *from* it. I was walking in it for longer periods of time. As a situation would present itself, I was responding from this authentic place, and it felt so right; so real. I was letting go of the old me, and embracing the reality of this wonderfully fitting me.

Oh, I still throw on my ill-fitting me plenty of times; the me whose buttons get easily pushed, who is quick to anger, and whose ego is easily bruised. To this point in my life that continues to be part of my human experience, and I see it as a way for me to know where there is more work to be done.

But, my understanding is anchored now in knowing that the Stillness within *is* who I am. At the level of Spirit I have always been this, and now I have begun experiencing it at the level of my consciousness. This is the Feminine rising in me.

SECTION THREE

The Feeling Tone of Spirit

CHAPTER SIX

How About Those Feelings?

I was introduced to the term "the feeling tone of Spirit" while participating in the Prosperity Plus...A New Way of Living course offered by Mary Manin Morrisey. For me, this term expresses an excellent way to recognize Spirit, and so I humbly share the phrase and what it means to me, here with you.

Feelings - we spend a whole lot of time trying not to have some of them, and trying to have more of others. We're told not to trust our feelings; they are fickle, fleeting. And it sure seems like our feelings toss us about viciously at times. Should we listen to our heads, or our hearts, and why don't they match up more of the time?

All of this emotional turmoil is just another symptom of our unbalanced state. Our emotions are simply the product of our thoughts, experienced in our body. So, when our thoughts are unstable, our emotions are unstable, and our body systems are destabilized. It is from this compromised state that we are attempting to function on a daily basis.

Unlike our teetering emotions, the divinely balanced Feminine is not reactive to life's situations, She is responsive. This is an important distinction. As we allow the Feminine to rise up within us, we are coming out of our head, and into our Essence. You might call this your heart for geographic purposes.

The more we allow for Her response, the less we are carried away by our reactive thoughts, and the less emotional turmoil we experience. The more we are attuned to Spirit's voice, the more stable our life experience becomes.

I've been speaking about Spirit's voice throughout this book. Without having named it, we've been exploring the feeling tone of Spirit. It cannot be named with words. It is, at best, the inner response, perhaps elicited by the intention behind a word. Consider the difference you feel when you say, "war and peace", and "inner peace". An even easier distinction might be the different feeling tone between hate and love.

Should these examples not help you fully grasp the concept of feeling tones, there is one absolute identifier. Regardless of the specific feeling, the underlying tone of Spirit is stillness. Look beneath any of the feelings you may have, and if they are from Spirit, you will find an underlying sense of amazing stillness.

There are lots of other words you could layer on top of stillness. Peace, love, bliss, excitement, compassion, joy. But we can mimic all of those feelings in our humanness. The one we cannot fake is stillness. So, it becomes very easy to determine our current state of awareness. Is there stillness at its center?

This becomes an important marker to watch for, because as we attune ourselves to the Divine Feminine, we *can* begin to mimic Her. We can put on the mask, it's fast and easy. For a short-term issue, we can fake our way through it. But, if our work is authentic, we will want to check for the stillness. If we do not find it, we know what to do now. Go within to find Her.

Let me lovingly remind you again, if there are times you consciously or unconsciously choose to fake your way through a situation, through a day, or a month, please do not judge yourself.

Whenever you become aware that you have been carried away by your thoughts, or when you are ready to again engage with your practice, simply bring your awareness back to the Feminine, back to Spirit. Return to your practice without judgment, and your path with be clear for moving forward.

Attuning Ourselves to the Feeling Tone of Spirit

Experiencing the stillness I am speaking of here may take some focused practice on our part. Many of us are moving at such lightning speeds that any sense of stillness would be obliterated by our own sonic booms.

And I know for some of us, the idea of slowing down enough to experience stillness feels painful, even unappealingly dreadful. If that is your response, and you've gotten this far into my book, then you may be more ready for stillness than you think. I encourage you to take the time to find the stillness once. Then, you decide if it is worth experiencing more often.

For others, the mere mention of the word stillness elicits a deep, inner longing. If you look within that longing, you will find the stillness I speak of.

Most of us will need to sit quietly at first to experience this stillness of Spirit. Even when we've quieted our bodies, our minds are still running thoughts like the New York Stock Exchange ticker. This is why we meditate, or spend time in Nature. Until we become more accustomed to the feeling tone of Spirit, of the Balanced Feminine, we may only be able to experience this stillness when we are at our quietest.

I consider this a gift God offers our bodies and our psyches. The gift of slowing down, of quiet, of rest. Our modern society tells us we must be on the go all of the time. The Feminine shows us there is good work to be done in the stillness.

Now that we have a sense of what the feeling tone of Spirit is, let's anchor this concept by touching on what it is not. The Balanced Feminine will never bring a sense of "dis-ease" of any kind. Not unhappiness, not anxiety, not fear. Even Her response to tragedies and injustices are not from a foundation of sadness or righteous anger, but from compassion.

For a time we will still have our human reactions to things we see, or to things that happen in our lives. But we can check them right away. Go within. Listen for Her. You will know you have reached where She dwells when you sense Her peacefulness, Her ease, Her love. Double-check it for the stillness beneath what you are sensing.

When you do look within for your Divine response, what you find may be very different from your initial human reaction. The question then becomes, are you ready to release your old pattern of thinking and being, and expand your experience? The response of the Balanced Feminine is perfect. No arguing on our part will sway Her. Even our best argument is superficial compared to the wisdom of the Divine.

There is another way of being, and She offers to guide us there. This new way of being allows our responses to be clearly defined, confident, and effective. Even when responding to...perhaps especially when responding to, those tragedies and injustices appearing in our lives.

Being Trained in the Feeling Tone of Spirit

The feeling tone of Spirit is not altogether unfamiliar to those who seek Divine guidance through prayer, meditation, or other means. We often experience a strong sense of love and peacefulness during our spiritual supplications. Remember, the Divine Feminine is one aspect of God, so of course She feels familiar. But, we're beginning to expand our understanding of Her now. We have found our true inner home, our authentic personality.

Now we are learning what *living* from this space feels like. We have been conditioned to trust the thoughts in our mind, and react from there. It can take some practice to instead, see with our hearts, and allow our own Inner Wisdom to influence our mind's response. So, the work here is to get accustomed to how we experience things differently when we check in with our Divine Essence.

The feeling tone of Spirit is a graciously easy marker as we begin this work. It is as simple as asking how the Balanced Feminine feels about things that happen in our lives. It is akin to the question, "What would Jesus do?"

Like, when the neighbor is mowing their lawn at 6:00 a.m. on a Saturday, or when your child hasn't returned on time from being with friends. What is the response of the Feminine within when you think your partner is being dishonest, unfair, or reckless? Or when your boss is mean, or your employees are inconsiderate? How does the Divine Feminine respond when you have an important decision to make, or a difficult thing to say to someone?

If we can start with forgiving the person or situation, allowing for what is happening, we will have created good space for experiencing our Divine response. After that, check in with the Feminine to consider what is happening, and what the course of action is to be taken.

As we consciously look within for the possible responses, options, or ideas, there will be a feeling tone to each of them. This is when it gets real easy. We don't need to evaluate each idea or option, mull over the potential repercussions, or agonize over which way is right. We only need to do one thing. Find the one that has within it an undeniable stillness.

If a circumstance has you carried away with strong emotions, so that you cannot sense deeply enough to experience stillness, start another way. Scan your options for one that gives you even an inkling of peace, of renewal, of confidence, or ease. Look for one that gives you *life*, or one that lands with a "Yes!" Get the idea?

Once you have landed on an option that brings with it something resembling the feeling tone of Spirit, bring your awareness to it. Allow it to help you dive deeper within until you can sense stillness. If the option you've landed on does not assist you in this process, then consider the strong possibility it is not Spirit's response, and go back to the other options you were considering.

Very often it will be a much easier experience, especially with practice. It's possible we may simply know exactly what we need to say or do the moment we look within. That knowing will come with feelings of strength and fortitude. That knowing sits in our core like no decision we've ever made from our unconscious mind.

If we're not experiencing that knowing, we may be in our own way a bit. We can then click through the options as we see them, and note the feeling tone we experience with each one.

Let's consider that neighbor who is mowing their lawn at 6:00 a.m. on a Saturday. You are suddenly wakened by the grinding roar of the mower only feet from your bedroom window. If you are not able to see clearly from your heart in that moment, click through the options you might be considering. Notice how each one feels. Remember, you are looking for the feeling tone of Spirit.

> Option #1 - Kill your neighbor. How does that feel? (Okay, I know at first glance that might sound appealing, but the only way you get a "yes" for that one is when you are *not* standing in the light of the Divine.)
>
> Option #2 - Yell at your neighbor. How does that feel?

Option #3 – Allow for the moment, forgive your neighbor, and see what there is for you to learn, know, or experience in this. How does that feel?

The feeling tone shifts with Option #3, *if* we've come out of our heads, and looked into our hearts. Were you aware of it just now as you read? This can take practice, so if you don't feel the difference right away, it's okay.

The important thing to recognize is there is another place where we can experience ourselves. We can derive the interpretations of our experiences from our vacillating mind, and react as we always have. Or, we can shift our awareness to the Stillness within, and interpret our experiences from there.

Whenever we shift from mind-reacting to Spirit-responding, we invite expansion. That single act of seeking the Divine creates enormous space for the Balanced Feminine to rise and expand within us.

One practice that helps to drive our awareness directly to our Inner Guidance when situations arise is to immediately ask, "What am I to know, learn, or experience from this?" You can simplify that by asking, "What am I to know here?" Go within to see with your heart. There will be answers there. You will have created space for experiencing your Divine response.

It isn't more complicated than that. It's *supposed* to be easy! Divine Wisdom dwells within us. It is our very essence. That "still small voice", the knowing because we know, is evidence that this Wisdom dwells within us. We are *meant* to know. Divine Wisdom is one of the faculties we came into this life with. We simply have not been taught to pay attention to It, and so we have not learned to trust It.

As we attune ourselves to that still small voice, we will find It does not remain small. It becomes our ever-present compass, our ethereal Google, easily accessed, and clearly heard. Remember, It comes with very distinct feelings of peacefulness, confidence, and the tell-tale stillness. As we grow accustomed to listening for our Divine response, we learn to trust this Inner Guidance.

So now, let's glimpse back at the neighbor mowing at 6:00 a.m. The day you find yourself surrounding that person with loving energy, will be a day of true healing. That may not be all you do, but it can be the initial essence of your response. The neighbor may very well continue mowing, but I promise you something big will have happened.

You will have freed yourself from your old way of clogging up your heart with anger, or thoughts of revenge. You will have broken your pattern of stuffing your resentment, and then feeling guilty about it, or feeling badly about yourself for not being strong enough to do something about it.

Instead, you will have ignited a circle of healing. What impact that has on your neighbor may remain unknown to you. What comes next for *you* can get pretty exciting. Stay with this practice. It is so worthwhile.

So, we've now explored how the feeling tone of Spirit is not like the emotions we struggle with daily. It can be as simple as an inner yes, or no. The yes gives us positive feelings, peaceful, grounded feelings, with a foundation of stillness. And, the no....doesn't. It's that easy.

The fun part is, we begin to *know*. It feels safe. The ground beneath our feet feels solid in this place of knowing. No longer threshed about by our wavering emotions, we walk confidently, gratefully, and even joyfully.

Things that happen in our lives might still carry our human emotions away for a time, especially those things we perceive as big. Whenever you realize that has happened for you, forgive your human self for taking over the show, and return your awareness

Chapter Six: How About Those Feelings?

to the Divine within you. Ask, "What is meant for me to know here?" Dive deep within until you meet the Divine Feminine. She is always there, each and every moment, existing as the Stillness within. We are always one with that Stillness. Sometimes we just need to dive down deep to experience It.

A storm raging over an ocean impacts the water only so deep. Beneath that magical depth, stillness remains. When a storm rages in our life, all it takes for us to experience Stillness is to bring our awareness to It. So, dive down as far as it takes to leave your reckless mind to its own, and race to that place of Stillness.

Pay attention to what you experience in this Inner Space. Give no energy to thoughts that would carry you away to chaotic, panicky, or fearful emotions. Those emotions aren't wrong. They just aren't helpful for the situation, for your growth, or for experiencing the Wise Woman response to what is going on.

Feelings Meditation

The purpose of this meditation is to get a sense of how we can more readily distinguish the feeling tone of Spirit from our own emotional state. We are getting in touch with our feelings at the body level. For some this may feel very subtle, for others it may feel a bit overwhelming. Doing this work will help bring it into balance, in any case.

Sit or lie comfortably, and close your eyes. This practice is short, so you shouldn't need to be concerned with falling asleep.

Think about something or someone you love. Or, think about your very favorite place. Find a thought that makes you smile, or laugh. Spend a little time soaking in this feeling. How good does it feel?

Now, consciously make note of *where* you feel that wonderful, good feeling. Where do you feel it in your body? If you are not able to answer that right away, return to the thoughts of that favorite person, place, pet, or thing. Let the feeling expand by spending more time with it. Give time for a "best moment" to emerge.

Our bodies always respond to our thoughts, so if you have difficulty feeling where you experience this, keep checking around your body with your awareness as you spend time with these happy, loving thoughts. Do you feel warmth in your chest, or deep in your stomach area? Look within until you sense where and how your body is responding to these pleasing thoughts.

This is likely where your body will experience Spirit's voice. Consider this a good place to check in with when you are discerning your emotional state. When there is a decision to be made, check in with this part of your body for your "yes".

Now, close your eyes again. This time, think of something unpleasant; something negative.

Spend just enough time here to feel where *that* happens in your body. (The intention has been set that this be a safe exercise for the purpose of your greater understanding, so feel safe in this work.) Once you have determined *where* in your body you feel this negative feeling, consider this to be where your body would experience "no" when you are seeking your Inner Guidance.

Close your eyes one more time, and surround yourself with love. Clear your space of the negative, and take in a good dose of love. If you have any difficulty thinking of something loving or peaceful, picture someone you love joining you to do this for you.

A few ideas for this might be to imagine your child at a young age toddling over to you with a flower in its hand for you. Or, picture your dog or cat curling into your lap; experience the love you feel for each other. Or perhaps, imagine angels appearing around you, each one emanating the pure love of God towards you.

Before getting up, take a moment to enjoy the gratitude that is coming up from within you.

CHAPTER SEVEN

Divine Decisions

We have now created a new foundation for our decision-making process. Without drama, or being paralyzed by fear, we can simply look within, experience our connection to the Balanced Feminine, and determine our Divine response.

As an example, let's say you have more than one job offer. Consider one of your options, and listen for the Feminine response; feel where it hits your body. Consider the other option, listen and feel again. One of them will give you a "Yes". If one of them doesn't, then consider it likely that you haven't hit on the option Spirit has in mind for you yet.

It's quite possible that as we look for our Divine response, we will be inspired to expand our thinking. If you come across a time when you do not get a "Yes" feeling to the options you are considering, try dreaming a bit. Think a little bit bigger. Keep thinking and dreaming bigger until you get a "Yes". Then, try *that* one on for size. Get used to the sense of excitement it brings.

You may find yourself thinking, "Really? I could do *that*? I mean, I'd love to, but...really?" Then, listen for that "Yes!" Remember, the yes feeling *is* Spirit in you expressing Itself through you. Trust that when Spirit is inspiring you with an idea, It also has a way of working it out.

Spend time with these inspired ideas. Bask in the feeling tone of them. Imagine yourself standing in the space where your inspired desire is realized. This is a sacred space. It offers you much valuable information. You are standing in the very spot where the inspired idea has reached its fulfillment. You are surrounded by all of the ideas, next moves, and wisdom it took to get you there. Be open to knowing these things. You are meant to know. They were never meant to be hidden. Knowing is who you are!

Allow for this wonderful growth. Your connection with Spirit is expanding, and the Divine Feminine is rising in you. You are beginning to experience the Wise Walk of the Balanced Feminine.

The Mundane Decisions

It's exciting to know we can be making life-altering decisions from a place of strength. It is just as important to take on our day-to-day decisions with wisdom and strength.

Do I let my child do this, or that? Do I let them have this thing they are asking for? Do I want to go out with that guy a second time? Do I want to take this class, or that class?

We, of course, are always free to make these kinds of decisions the way we always have, with varying levels of uncertainty, agonizing, and angst. That is who we are in our unbalanced state. Even when we take quick, decisive action from our unbalanced states, we are at best hopeful things will work out as we planned.

At worst, we second-guess every step we take, biting our nails, and putting out fires as we see them arise. We may stand at-the-ready to come up with Plan B, if our first run doesn't work out. Or, we may just give up as we face mounting obstacles. How peaceful does that reactionary existence feel?

The Wise Walk of the Balanced Feminine

We are, however, able to experience a whole new way of decision-making. The Feminine brings with Her a rock solid knowing. Her wisdom becomes ours, so that even those around us can have a sincere appreciation of the decisions we are making. They too experience the wisdom of our choices as we speak our new truth.

Unlike our old decision-making patterns of fear, confusion, wavering, and second-guessing, the Balanced Feminine within us speaks clearly, and with conviction. She says, "Yes!" with a flare of passion. She points us to a good way with a heart-centered longing. She also surely reveals to us, "Not that way" with feelings of constriction, heaviness, or sometimes a simple "No".

Sound too easy? Remember those paradigm shifts we talked about? This is one of those. Why is it supposed to be hard? It is time to tear up our agreements with experiencing our lives as difficult, with struggle, or as too hard. We can then make new agreements to experience our lives as gracefully simple, easy, and abundant.

Just try it on for size. Test it for yourself. See how this new way fits the next time you are faced with a decision to make. Consider one of the choices before you. How does that option make you feel as you check within? Do you get a full-body yes? Does it feel life-giving?

Consider another, or the other choice. How does that option make you feel? Look inside. Does your throat feel a little tighter as you think of one? Do you feel yourself contract inside? Does your heart feel constricted with one of the options? Those are your "not this way", "this ain't it" clues. Keep going until you find an option that gives you that Yes feeling.

Whether it be the day-to-day decisions, or the really big ones, once you find that Yes, trust It. If your old way of thinking pops in

Chapter Seven: Divine Decisions

and starts broiling up all its fears and doubts, return your awareness to the Feminine. Dive deep within to check for the knowing that came with the original Yes. In our newness, we may allow our excitement to cause us to surface too quickly from our journey within, and therefore miss experiencing the knowing that anchors our choice.

This knowing can be a challenge to describe. It is not always knowing what the outcome will be, although that may be true. It certainly is not always knowing the whole game plan. It is, however, absolutely knowing the next step to take. You are so certain of it, you don't feel the need to question it. You don't have to work yourself up to it; She brings that knowing. The Balanced Feminine *is* the part of you that knows, that has always known. *You've* always known what to do, and when to do it. You just need to bring your awareness to that part of you. The practice we are talking about here can help.

At first this may all feel like something too special, or too great for just anyone to experience. It *is* quite special. It is also absolutely how it is supposed to be for each of us. It is the most awesome thing, and the most natural thing. It is our intended way of being. Be grateful, and revel in it. You are getting acquainted with your Guru, and It is you.

Gratefully, as the Feminine rises within us, and we begin moving in our world using the Wisdom we possess, our ego no longer impacts our decision making the way it had been. As we release our old pattern of thinking, we create space for Spirit to fill us up with even more understanding of our true essence. We can experience our new way of seeing with our hearts. That is the Feminine rising.

As we consciously walk with Her, experiencing Her functioning within us, we begin walking with great confidence. We know without wavering what the next step is to take. We easily allow for lessons along the way.

We also know that our new way of decision-making might look a little different to those around us. Our level of confidence may look *really* different to those around us. I suppose, depending on whether we've let the Feminine rise up quietly, or with a big bang, we may need to allow for those around us to get accustomed to our new way of being.

We have begun to live consciously. At first, some of our strongest work may revolve around remaining conscious with those closest to us. This is good work to do. It strengthens our practice.

A beautiful thing happens as we bask in this cosmic breathwork of releasing old patterns and expanding to new ones. We don't concern ourselves so much with how our lives look to people. That sort of falls away, in part because this expansion feels so incredible. So, it's okay if people don't quite get it. Why should they? We didn't either…until we did.

> *"What other people think of me is none of my business."*
> - Eleanor Roosevelt

SECTION FOUR

Moving Forward

CHAPTER EIGHT

What if We were <u>All</u> Right?

In order to experience God in new ways, we may need to believe in new ways. Some of us may need to look beyond the constraints of our current religious beliefs and practices. This chapter offers a perspective on why that need not be a herculean feat.

Allowing for a New Path

We allow ourselves to make changes all the time when we become unsatisfied with what we are experiencing. We change jobs, cars, our hair color, our marital status. There is a glaring exception to that rule – religion/spirituality.

Should we find ourselves dissatisfied with, or unfulfilled by, our religious experience, few of us consider looking to other spiritual perspectives to find a better fit. We would sooner ignore our religion, or simply walk away from it, than explore other spiritual paths for one that would bring us life.

Many of us identify with our spiritual choice with an intensity that can be smothering. We are only allowed to breathe the air that comes with that religion. If we are not sustained by this air, we are destined to limp along, one labored breath at a time, as our religion metaphorically dies a slow death in our heart.

Others who become disenchanted with their religion often have to tear themselves away with a crushing sense of disillusionment, sometimes walking away from all aspects of spirituality. We tie so much to our religious experience. Right, wrong, life, death. When we have selected a religious belief, all other choices become wrong. In almost no other aspect of life do we put that kind of burden on ourselves, or each other.

A Different Perspective

What if we were all right? What if there was no wrong path to take? I am no expert in the field of world religions, but I am at least quite familiar with one of the most popular in the United States. So, I think I will be effectively reflecting the view of a great number of people with the statement below.

Many a spiritual practice includes the belief of an omnipresent God, with some choosing another name for this Essential Being. So, God existing everywhere, present *in everything*. That would include God existing *in* every single person.

From that perspective, we should have no qualms between differing religious beliefs. God is *successfully* existing in all things. The Divine wasn't somehow squeezed out of those who have chosen to believe something different from us. And, *you* don't have to abandon God because the religion you have been practicing is no longer serving you, or never did.

A spiritual or religious practice can simply be viewed as a preferred way of experiencing our connection with the One Source. Whatever we believe at this time is what we need to believe in order to move forward in our spiritual growth.

The same is true for those who believe differently from us. They have not chosen a wrong path, only a different one. Even those "crazy" atheists. God not exercising belief in God? Some might find that a wonderful way of creating space for new understanding.

With this God-in-all perspective, we can then trust that God, existing in each of us, is leading us perfectly well on the right path.

Changing Paths

When we see someone we care about in a job that stifles them, makes them unhappy, or doesn't fulfill them, we encourage them to consider finding one that will bring them fulfillment. Armed with our new perspective, we can now encourage someone to explore another *spiritual* path when we witness them trudging along their current one, unfulfilled, unhappy, never progressing, or growing.

We can do the same for ourselves, as well. If we allow for choice being akin to growth, then we need not abandon one religion, or spiritual perspective for another. We can, simply and easily, move from one path to another as we continue our spiritual walk.

This does not mean we were wrong before, or those still on the other path are wrong. It does not mean we now have the *real* truth. We are simply moving in the direction that is right for us at this time. Having taken this new path, we will learn new skills and different ways of thinking about things. It's very much the same as when we take on a new job. We'll have new things to learn, many of which will bring about new growth in us.

Religious Languages

As another way to shift our perspective, consider for a moment the concept of our various spiritual practices being likened to speaking different languages. It then simply becomes the way we express ourselves spiritually.

We don't feel a need to make the rest of the world speak our personal language, do we? We never feel inclined to hurt someone because they speak a language different from our own. We have no animosity towards someone because they speak Italian, for example. As a matter of fact, when we hear a different language that sounds appealing to us, we might just decide to learn to speak that language, too.

To bring this point home, consider what we are doing when we learn another language. We're finding out how someone else says something differently from the way we say it.

So then, if we looked at our spiritual expressions as languages, perhaps we'd be saying things like, "I *speak* Christian", instead of, "I *am* Christian". Instead of saying she *is* Jewish, we would say she *speaks* Jewish...he speaks Muslim, they speak Hindi. And then, we might just consider asking, "What word do *you* use for God?" Perhaps we could engage in extraordinary conversations of learning this way.

One Way of Seeing the Truth of This

Consider the way a child might draw the sun on a piece of paper-a big yellow ball with yellow arms reaching out from the ball in all directions. Each of those yellow arms is completely, and fully of the sun. All the arms are equally an aspect of the sun.

If these rays of sun were to be called individual names (religions), they would still be equally of the sun. And, if each of these rays called the sun something other than the sun, they would all still be pointing to that yellow ball, and they would all still have come from that yellow ball.

In the following paragraph, I am choosing to use the word God. Please insert the word you recognize to describe this Essential Being.

Back to the yellow sun. This is our relationship to God. We are each completely, and fully of God. We can't *be* anything other than that. We are each here on Earth as a ray of God. All equal rays, irrespective of what we are calling ourselves, and of our beliefs. We may have succeeded in creating an *illusion* of separation between us by taking on these religious identities, but we are no less each a ray of God. We cannot be otherwise.

Taking on this perspective, we are now free to explore different expressions of spirituality. If your current spiritual choice gives you life, if you feel your consciousness expanding within the practices you now enjoy, that is fantastic. Remain open to God for what else you might find fulfilling.

If, however, you feel a pull to something more, or feel constricted by your current spiritual practices and beliefs, or you have no spiritual practice, allow yourself to explore any number of spiritual languages. Trust your Inner Guidance to lead you to where you will experience expansion, greater awareness, and consciousness. Find the expression of God that fits what you feel within.

CHAPTER NINE

Where can We Go from Here?

When we have tapped into our True Essence, we have reached the inner well of Endless Supply. We have found our spiritual gold. Instead of refining what we have mined, It will refine us. We only need to honor and allow for this beautiful process.

As each of us begins our Wise Walk of the Balanced Feminine, we are joining with the stream, this layer of consciousness called the Balanced Feminine. And what a quantum leap in consciousness She brings to the way we experience our life.

As more of us tap into this well of consciousness, we expand this Feminine flow of awakening. We are ushering in a new phase to our woman's movement; one that truly liberates us. The Wise Woman's movement, the Femin*ine* movement!

Where *can* we go from here? Wherever we want to go. As the Feminine rises within me, my heart's desire will pull me to what is right for me. Your heart's desire will draw you to what is right for you, as the Feminine rises within you. Our desires will continue to be different, but each of us will become masterful at manifesting those desires.

The shift will not be in *what* we are doing, but *how* we will be doing it. We will be moving in our world with what is now an uncommon wisdom, caring for ourselves and those around us with what is now an uncommon sense of balance. We will be creating with what is now an uncommon power to create, walking with an uncommon knowing, experiencing and sharing a currently uncommon joy.

How we live these lives we consciously choose will be evidence of our liberation from old paradigms. We will no longer be thrashing about in the sea of stereotypes, desperate to find our footing, our purpose, our true self. We'll no longer be clawing at our sisters in jealousy, and mistreating each other in unconscious competition.

Liberating ourselves, we can begin to live our natural and intended way of being. This means speaking our truth, grounded in our walk, wise in our words, strong, welcoming, compassionate, creative, all with a foundation of unconditional love. We will experience our aliveness in a new way, and our consciousness will invite that awakening in others.

With every awakening, there is a widening of the stream of consciousness that is this phase of our woman's movement. As the Feminine rises in each of us, we add to this stream of healing energy, helping others to awaken more easily to *their* true Nature.

Releasing Our Hold on Unbalanced Energy

Coming into our own True Essence, we release our hold on the unbalanced energy we have been operating from. Part of what we are releasing is the unbalanced masculine energy we took hold of decades ago, during our feminist revolt.

Releasing our hold on unbalanced masculine energy, we become pivotal in creating space for the extraordinary Balanced Masculine energy to rise and expand to *His* intended way of being, both in us as women, and in those here as men.

It is here I bring those wonderful men, and our relationships with them, back into the picture. Whether it be our conscious choice to share our romantic lives with them or not, our relationship with the Divine Masculine will be restored to its intended balance.

From this space, we can coexist consciously at the human level, fully aware of our oneness, expressing the love of the Divine with, and for each other. Here, we are no longer separate from, and unknowable to each other.

Far removed from our Western culture that deems men unnecessary by some, in our balanced states we highly prize the value of the Balanced Masculine. We have a deep understanding and appreciation for the work and purpose of the Divine Masculine. Our freedom in expressing this gratitude and love allows for the Masculine to expand in His balanced state even further.

The Feminine, in turn, experiences how prized and honored Her purpose is by the Masculine. Each honors the absolute importance of the other, and recognizes that one is not better than the other. We are only different aspects of the One Source. And when we experience our connection at this level, we are able to coexist on the physical plane as intended, in love.

All our desires regarding relationships find fulfillment here. To stop playing games, to be loved completely, to feel validated, worthwhile, accepted for who we are, for passion, romance, and harmony. Here is where we begin to create this experience at the physical level.

Generations to Come

Our new consciousness will invite others to awaken. As we liberate ourselves from our limited thinking we leave signposts, markers, an energetic wake if you will. These make it easier for those in our lives, and the next generations, to find and walk within this space.

Chapter Nine: Where can We Go from Here?

We will begin to teach from within this harmonic flow of the Balanced Feminine. What is a new understanding for us becomes a natural way of being for our daughters, and their daughters. Who knows where the next generations will take this phase of our feminine movement? Wherever they want, if we have taught them the freedom that comes with the Wise Walk of the Balanced Feminine.

So woman, it's time to wake up. You are needed. We are the ones we have been waiting for!

Made in the USA
Middletown, DE
12 December 2020